Walking Awake

THE FACES IN NATURE

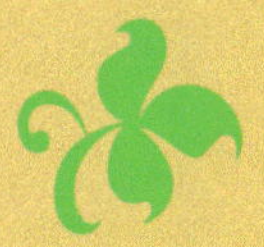

Denise Crawn

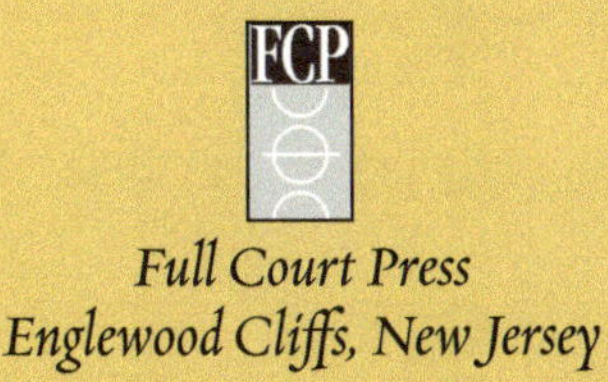

Full Court Press
Englewood Cliffs, New Jersey

First Edition

Published in the United States of America
by Full Court Press, 601 Palisade Avenue
Englewood Cliffs, NJ 07632
www.fullcourtpressnj.com

ISBN 978-1-938812-09-5
Library of Congress Control No. 2012955150

Editing and Book Design by Barry Sheinkopf
for Bookshapers (www.bookshapers.com)

Colophon by Liz Sedlack

This book is dedicated to the memory of my father,
Richard Charles Luke

HAVE YOU EVER WISHED that there was more to your surroundings than the obvious? Perhaps a secret code or message waiting for you to decipher? A special key designed just for you to help you find your way through the labyrinth of life? I believe that we are all surrounded by guides and signs to accompany us as we walk through life, in all that we do. I believe it is through these signs that we are reminded of our interconnectedness to All, if we can simply "walk awake." If you believe or wish, I have a story for you.

In my early teens, spending time with my father meant spending time in the woods. The years that we did—hunting, fishing, walking, talking, and sitting in silence—prepared me for life yet to come in immeasurable ways. This solid foundation has served as a special gift, which I have carried with me in all that I do. It has enhanced my intuition and, most importantly, taught me to see the true connectedness of all beings, nature, and Spirit. It was a feeling of "home" I would hold forever in my heart.

Not long ago, while going through a very difficult transitional period in my life, I felt a need to get back to nature to reconnect to my roots. I began to go for long walks in the woods. As I slipped into a meditative state, I would "sense" a "calling" to turn and look one way or another. Each time, I saw a reminder in nature that I was not alone on my journey. The "calls" came in forms of signs, such as hearts, or wings, or embracing trees, but also as what appeared to be "faces" in the trees and in the stones. My camera is often my companion on my journeys, so I began to photograph my new "friends."

Many of these photographs were taken in the forests, public parks, and hiking trails of Pennsylvania, New Jersey, and New York—some even in the heart of New York City! Others were taken while on pilgrimage to Canada, Scotland, and Ireland, and in sacred groves, near stone circles and other mystical places including the Isle of Iona, Scotland. I have chosen to keep their precise locations and "names" a secret not only out of respect for them, but also to challenge you.

There is an old saying: "You can't see the forest for the trees." In this book, I will take you to that forest, a primal place that offers a feeling of remembrance, of not being alone, of being connected with something larger than the human mind can envision. The trees remember. The stones remember. The stars remember. Do *you* remember? I ask you to take the time in your busy life to "walk awake"; go to the forest, look differently at the trees, the stones, the clouds, and the landscape. Listen, sense, find the companions and guides along your journey, and discover the messages awaiting you behind their "faces."

Welcome home!

—D.C.

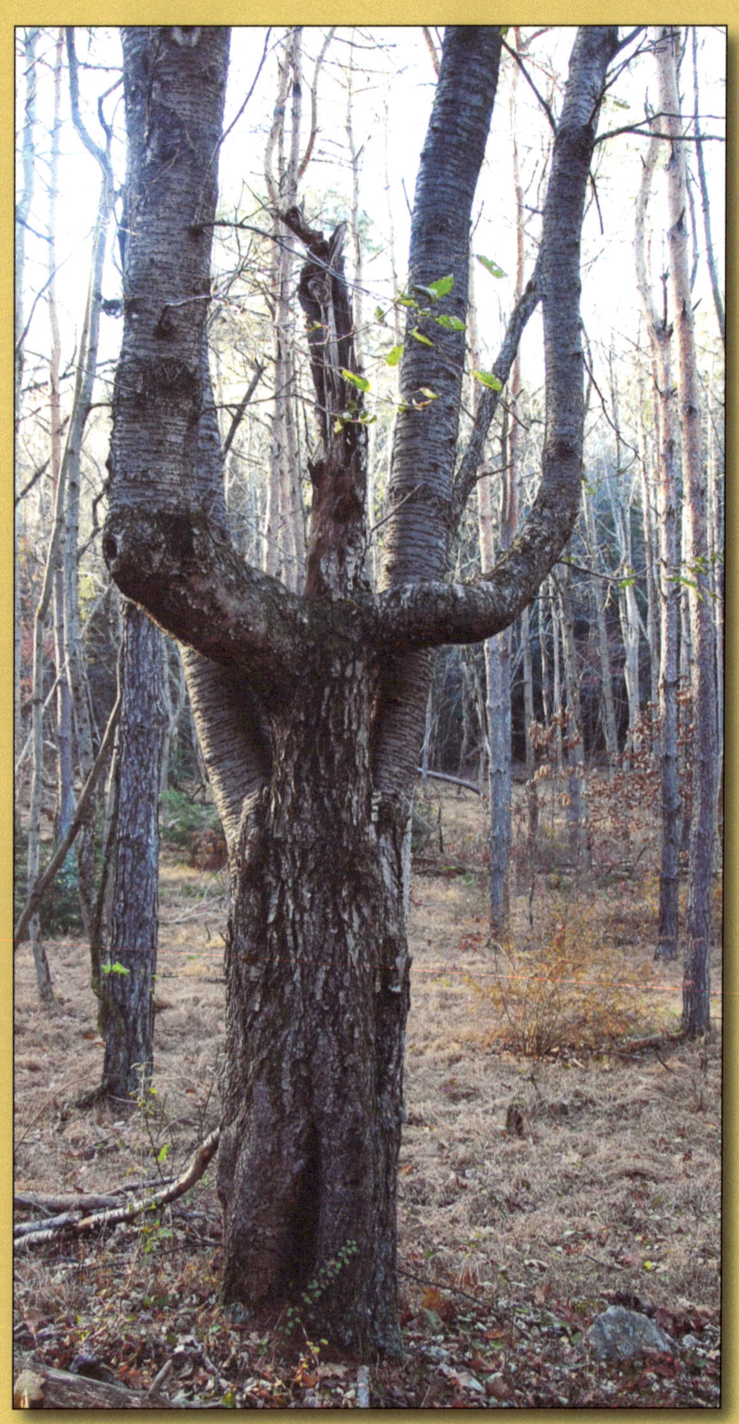

Nature

As a fond mother, when the day is o'er,
Leads by the hand her little child to bed,
Half willing, half reluctant to be led,
And leave his broken playthings on the floor,
Still gazing at them through the open door,
Nor wholly reassured and comforted
By promises of others in their stead,
Which, through more splendid,
may not please him more;
So Nature deals with us, and takes away
Our playthings one by one, and by the hand
Leads us to rest so gently, that we go
Scarce knowing if we wish to go or stay,
Being too full of sleep to understand
How far the unknown transcends
the what we know.

—Henry Wadsworth Longfellow

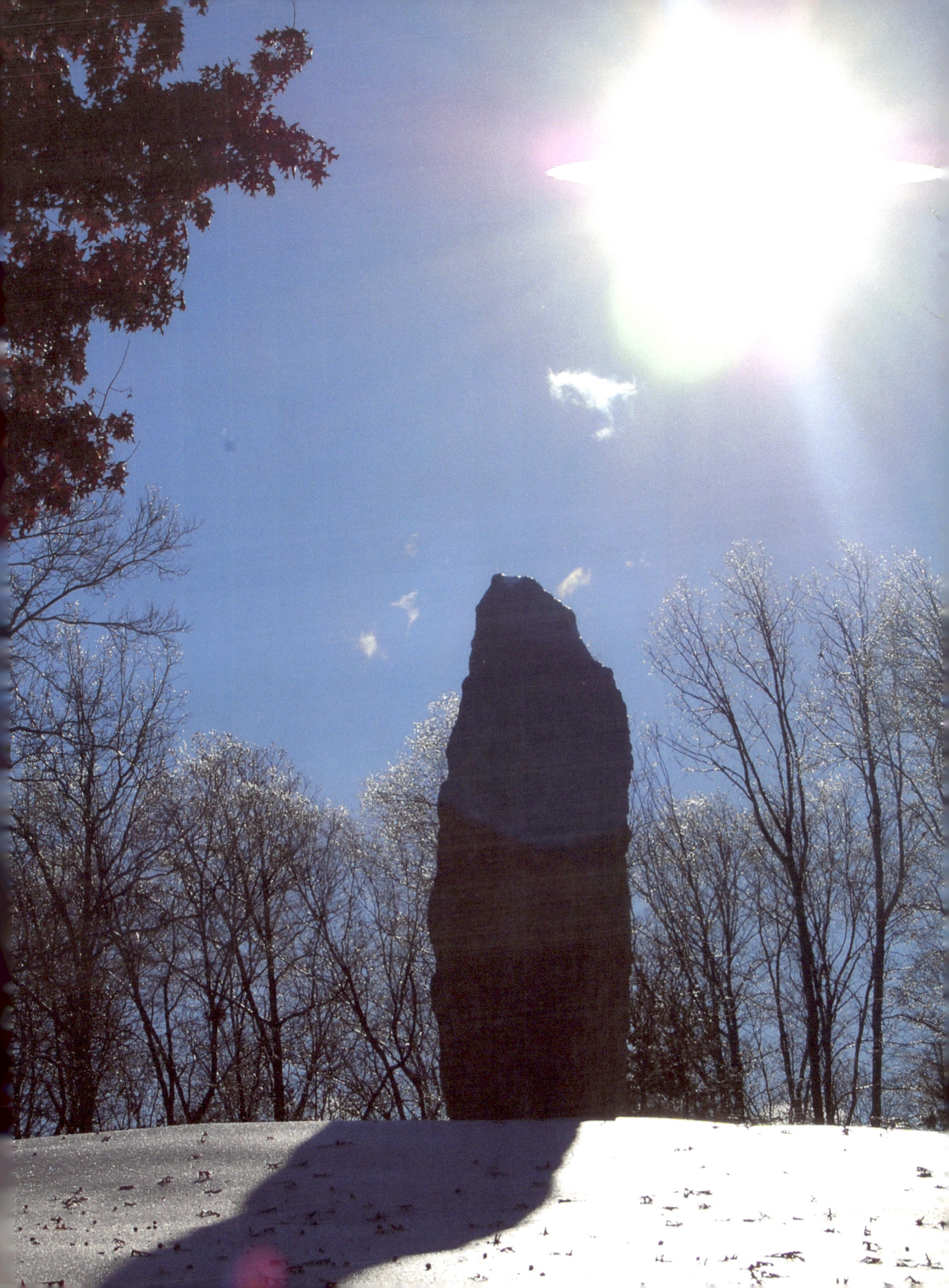

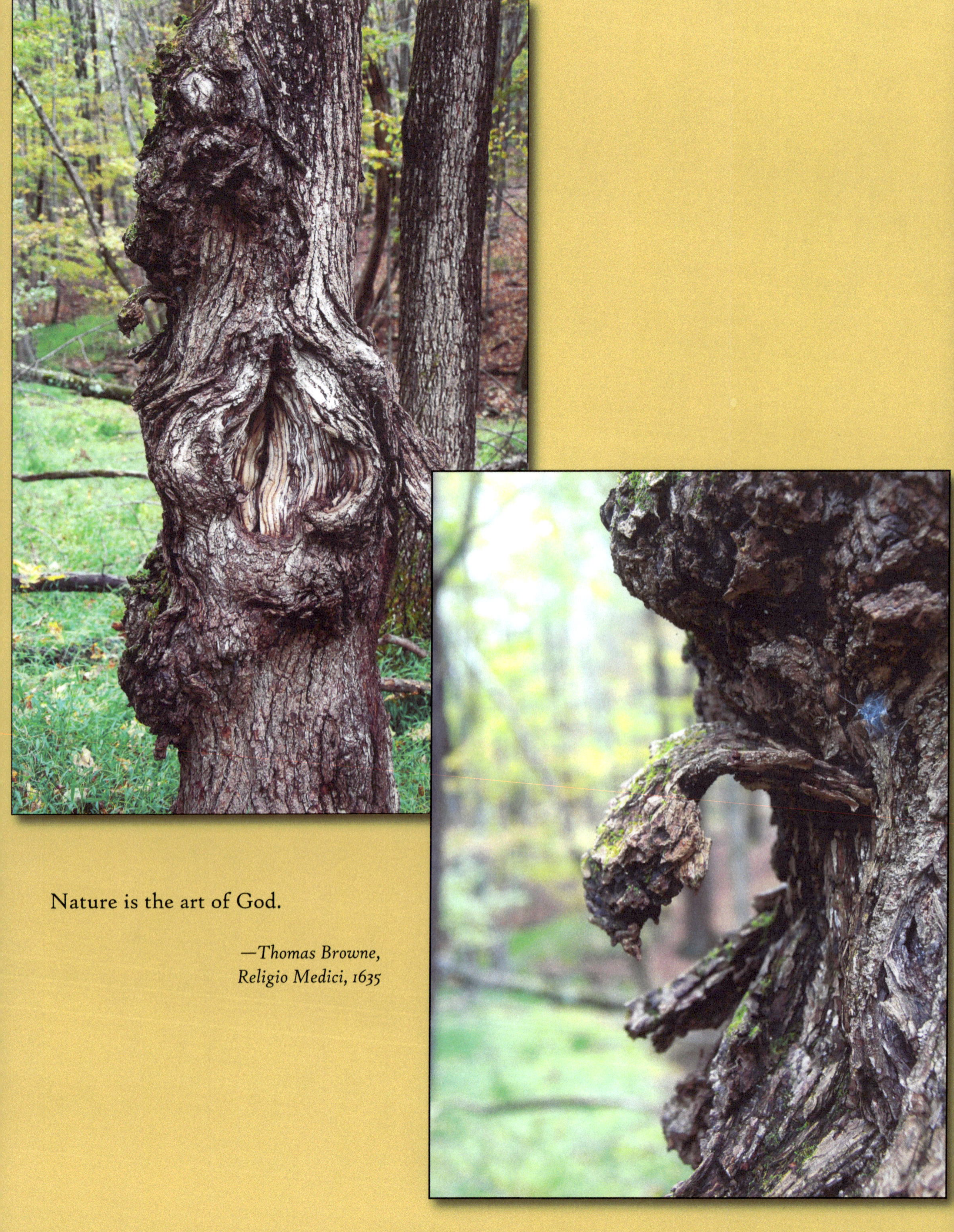

Nature is the art of God.

—*Thomas Browne, Religio Medici, 1635*

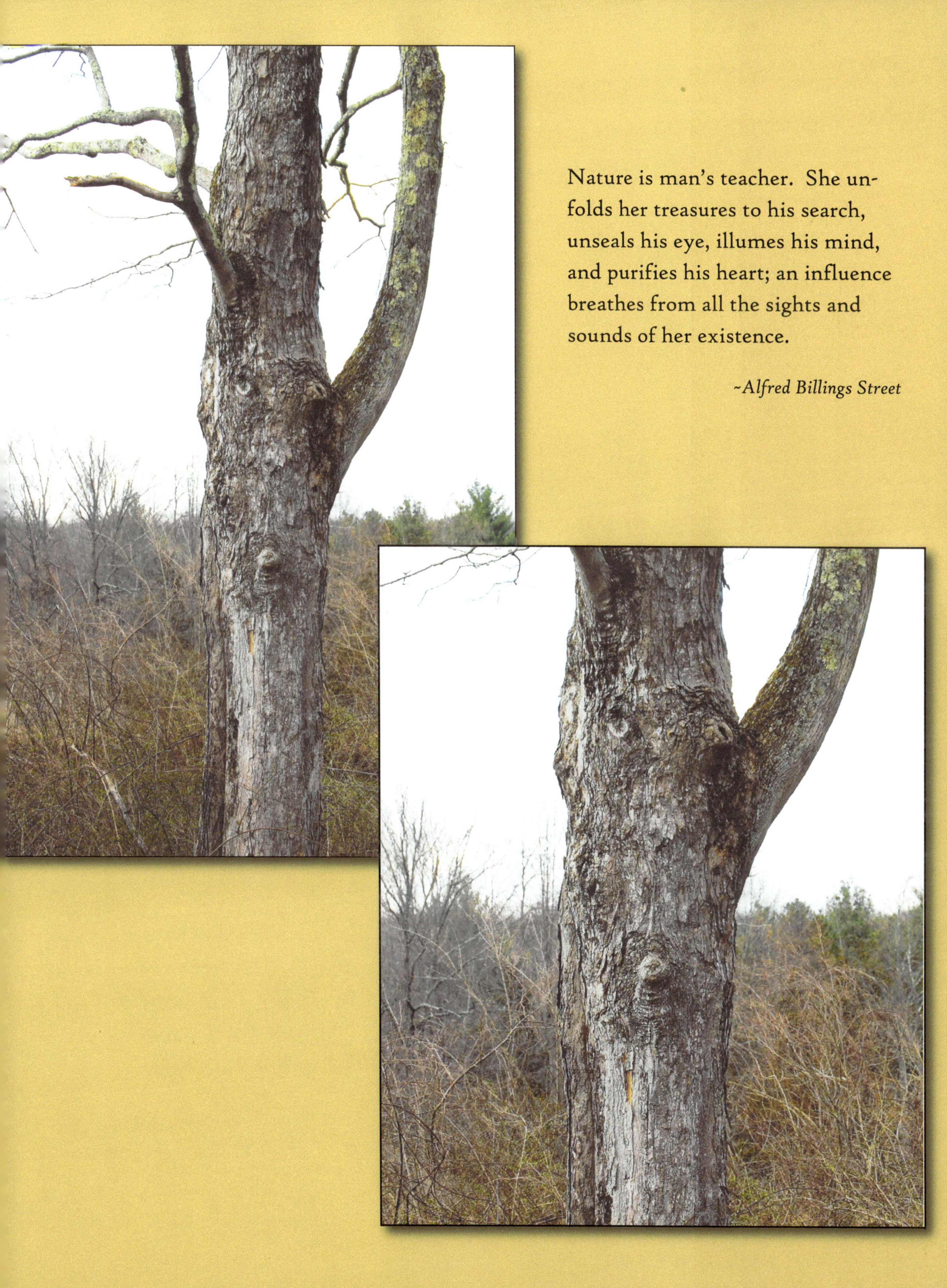

Nature is man's teacher. She unfolds her treasures to his search, unseals his eye, illumes his mind, and purifies his heart; an influence breathes from all the sights and sounds of her existence.

~Alfred Billings Street

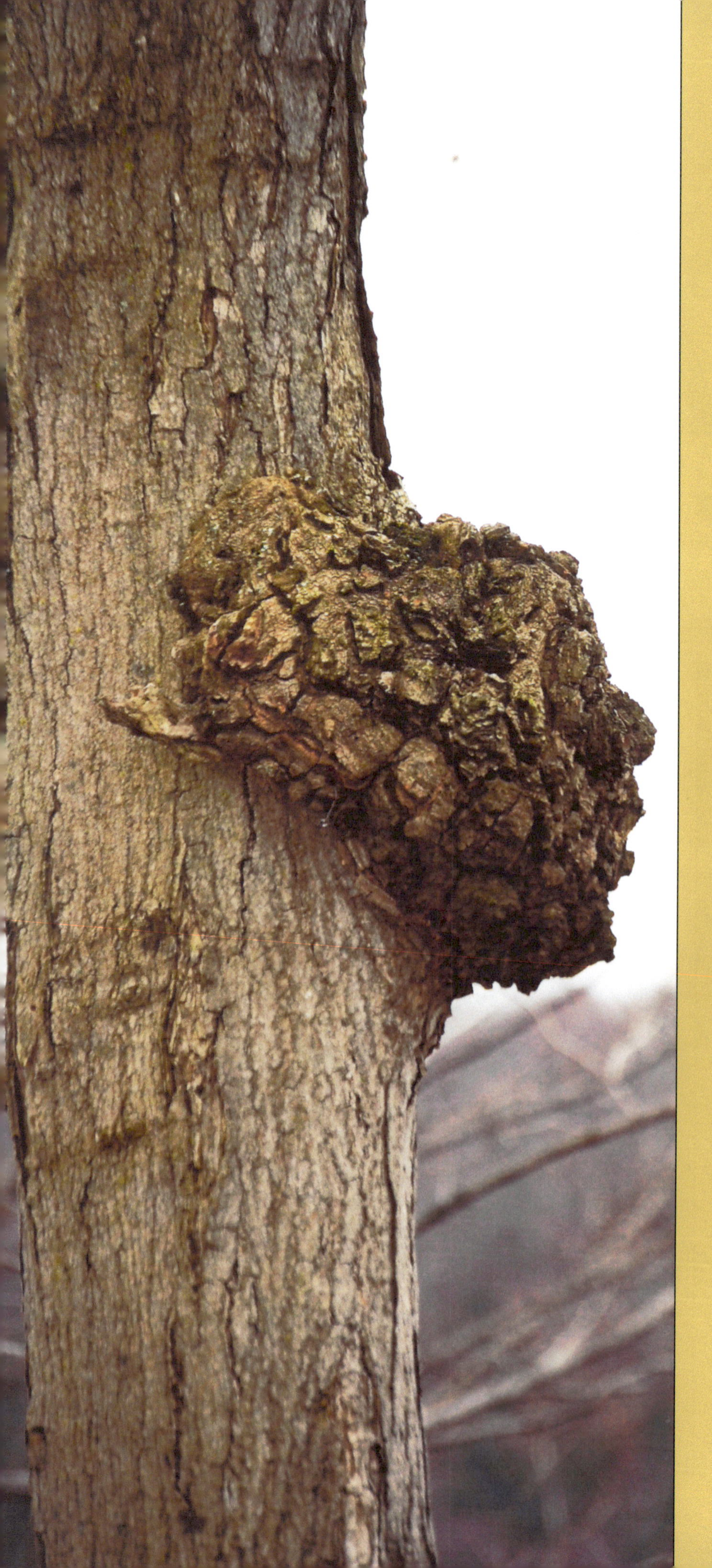

One impulse from a vernal wood
May teach you more of man,
Of moral evil and of good,
Than all the sages can.

—William Wordsworth,
"The Tables Turned," 1798

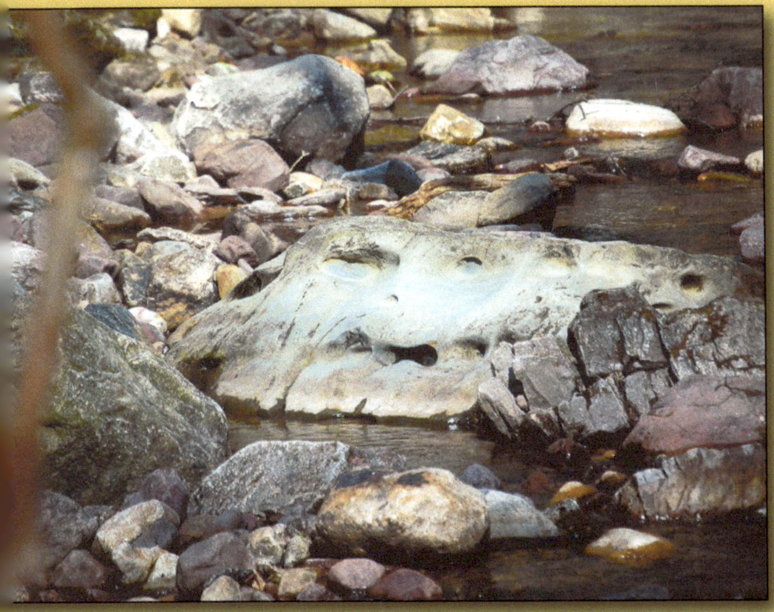

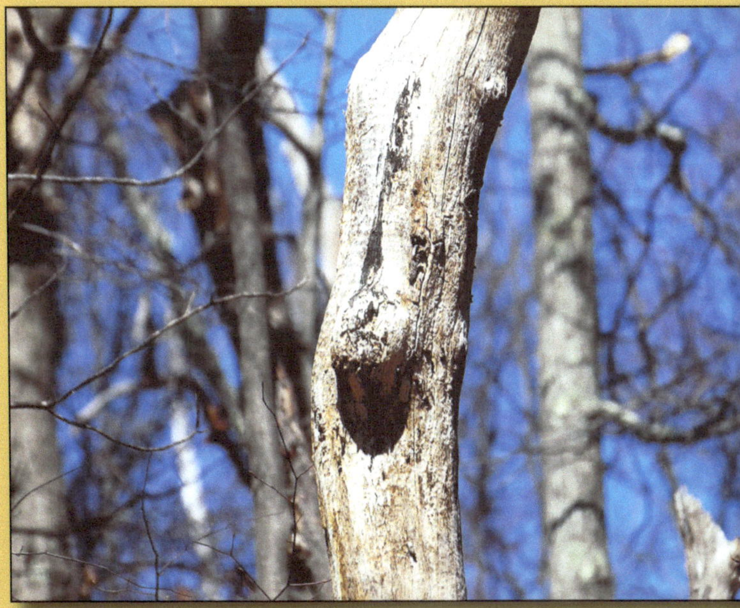

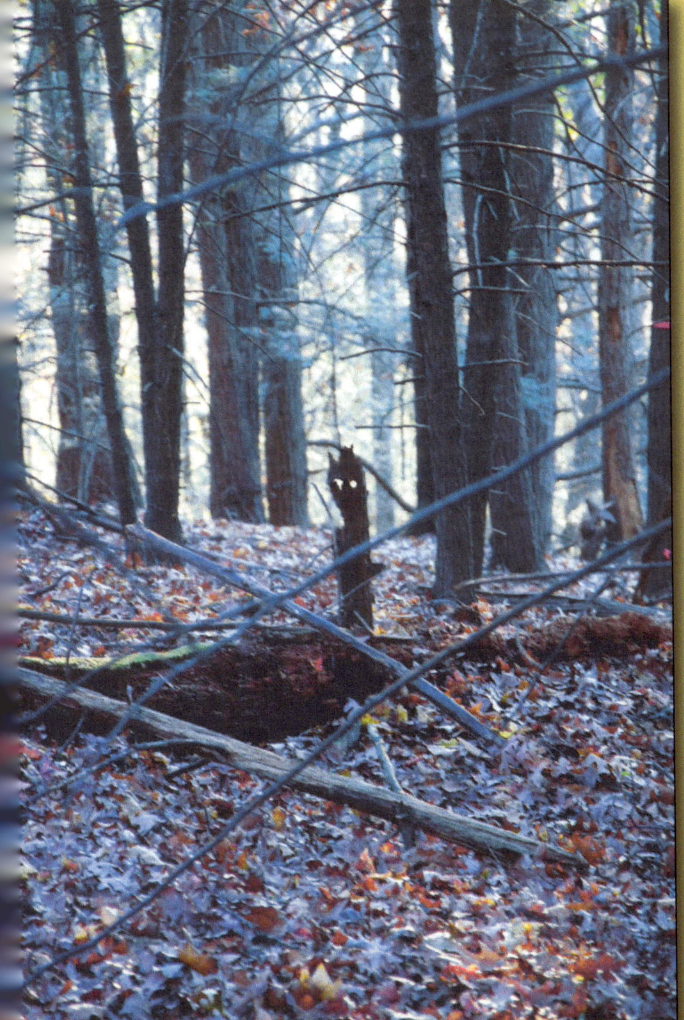

We abuse land because we regard it as a commodity belonging to us. When we see land as a community to which we belong, we may begin to use it with love and respect.

—*Aldo Leopold*

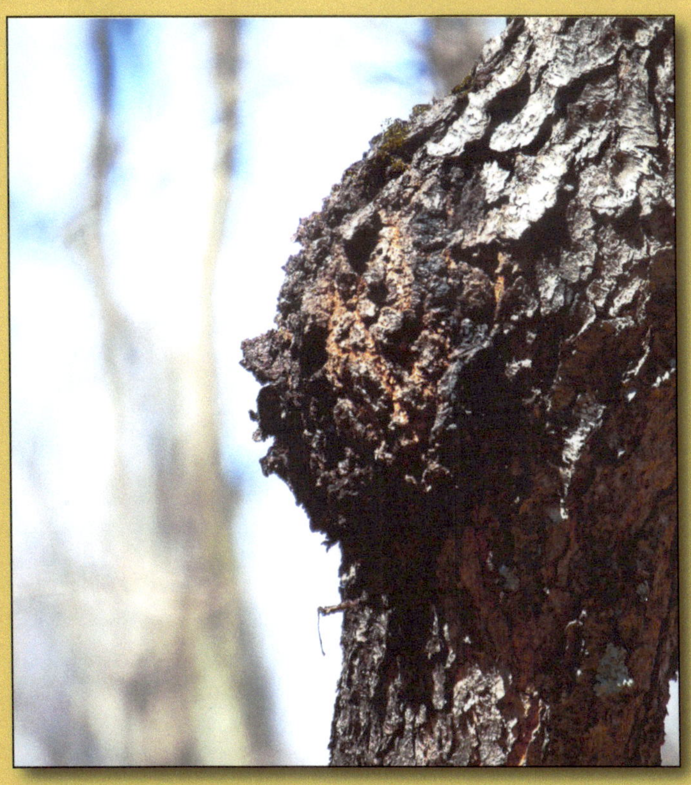

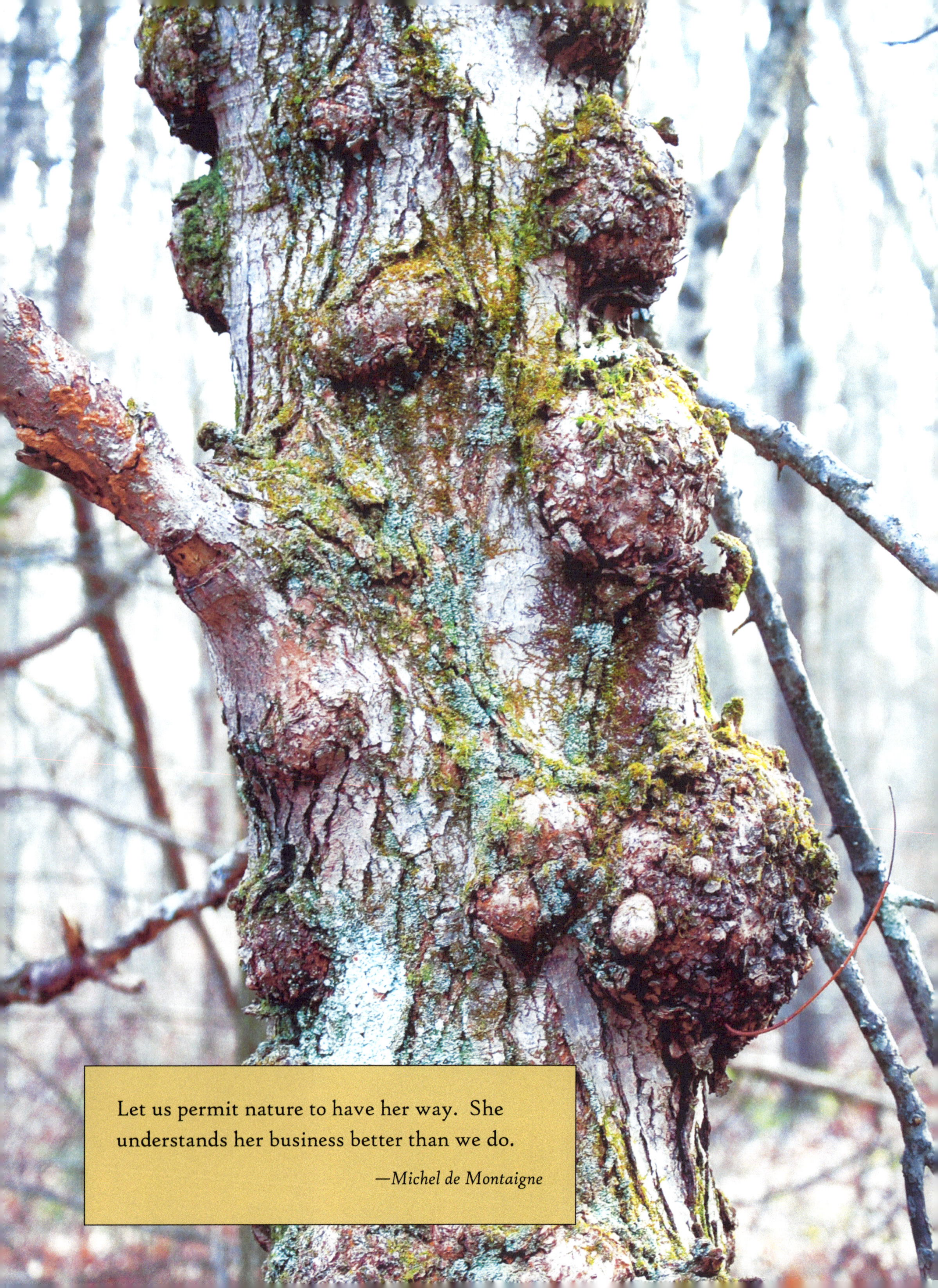

Let us permit nature to have her way. She understands her business better than we do.

—Michel de Montaigne

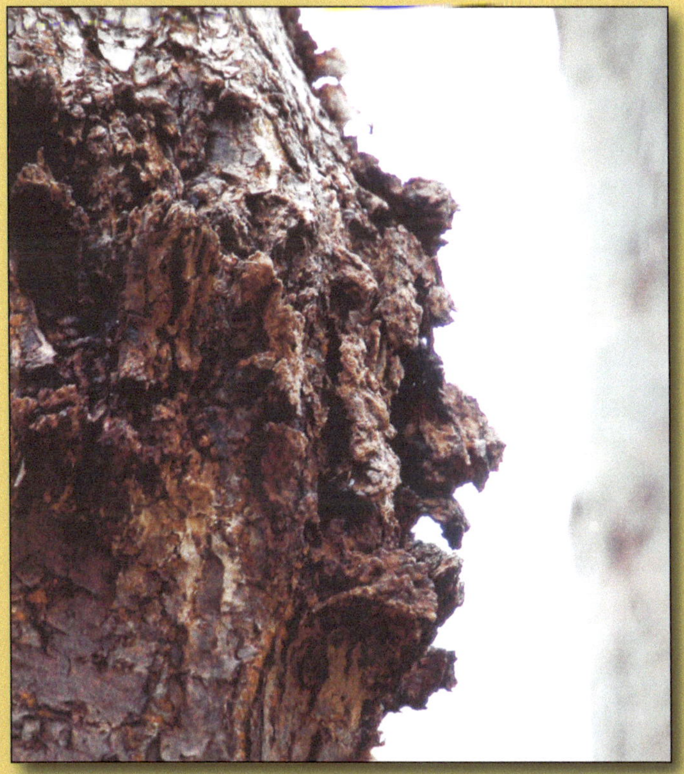
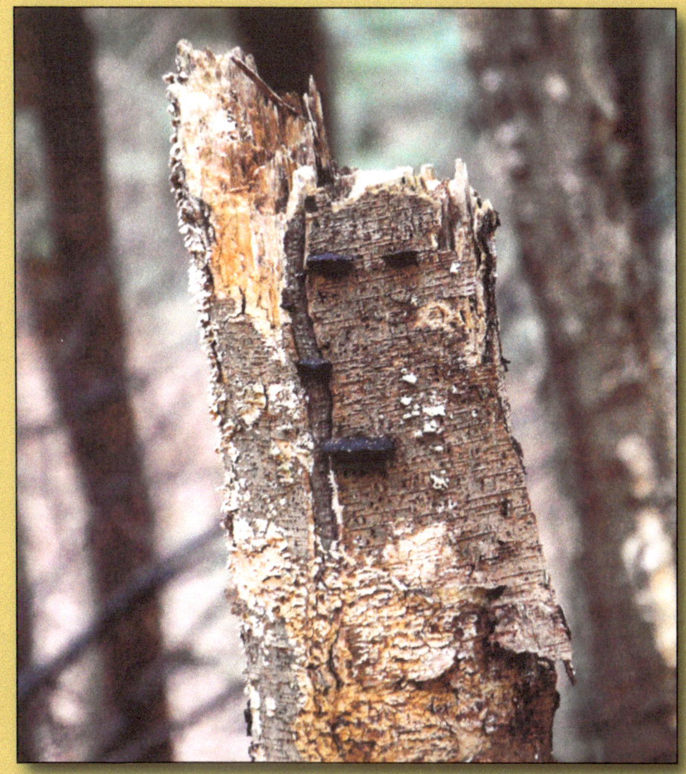
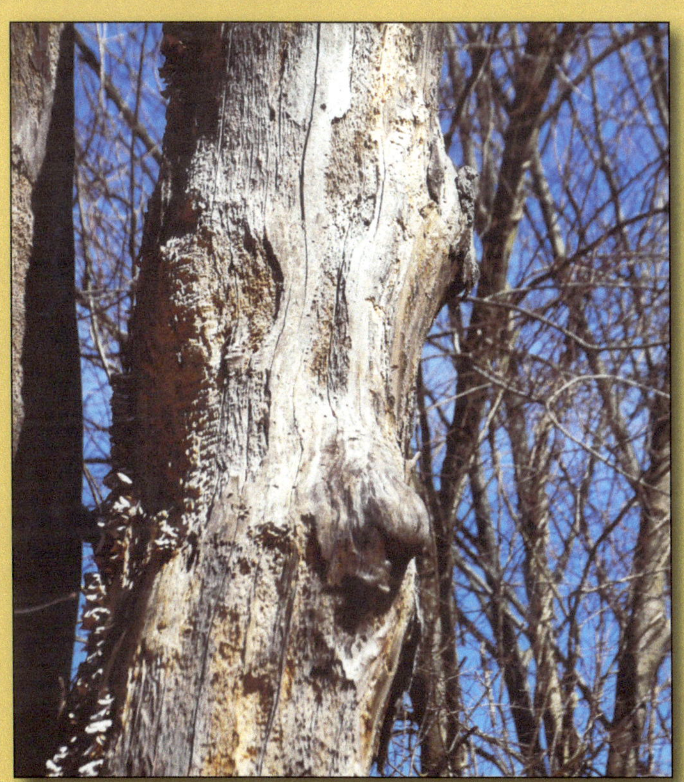
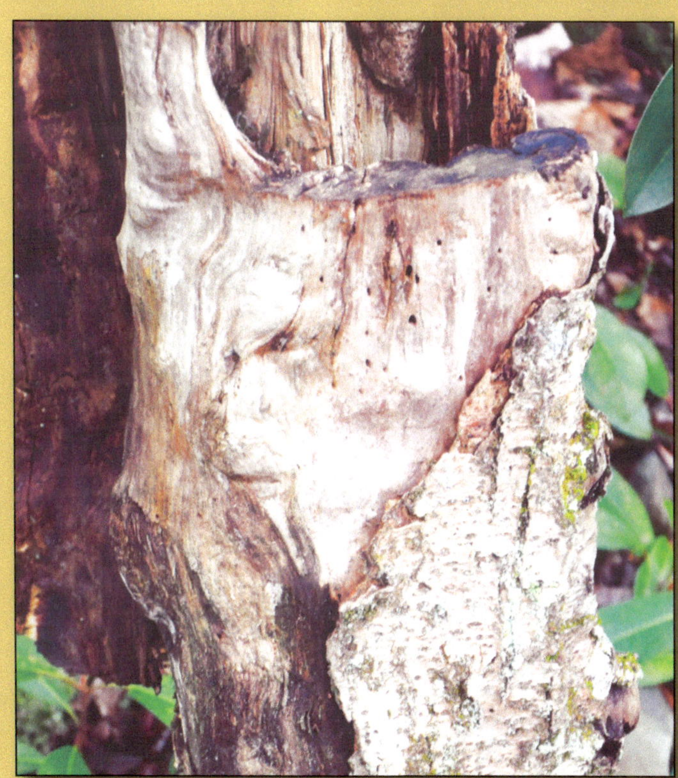

And this, our life, exempt from public haunt,
Finds tongues in trees, books in the running brooks,
Sermons in stones, and good in everything.

—William Shakespeare

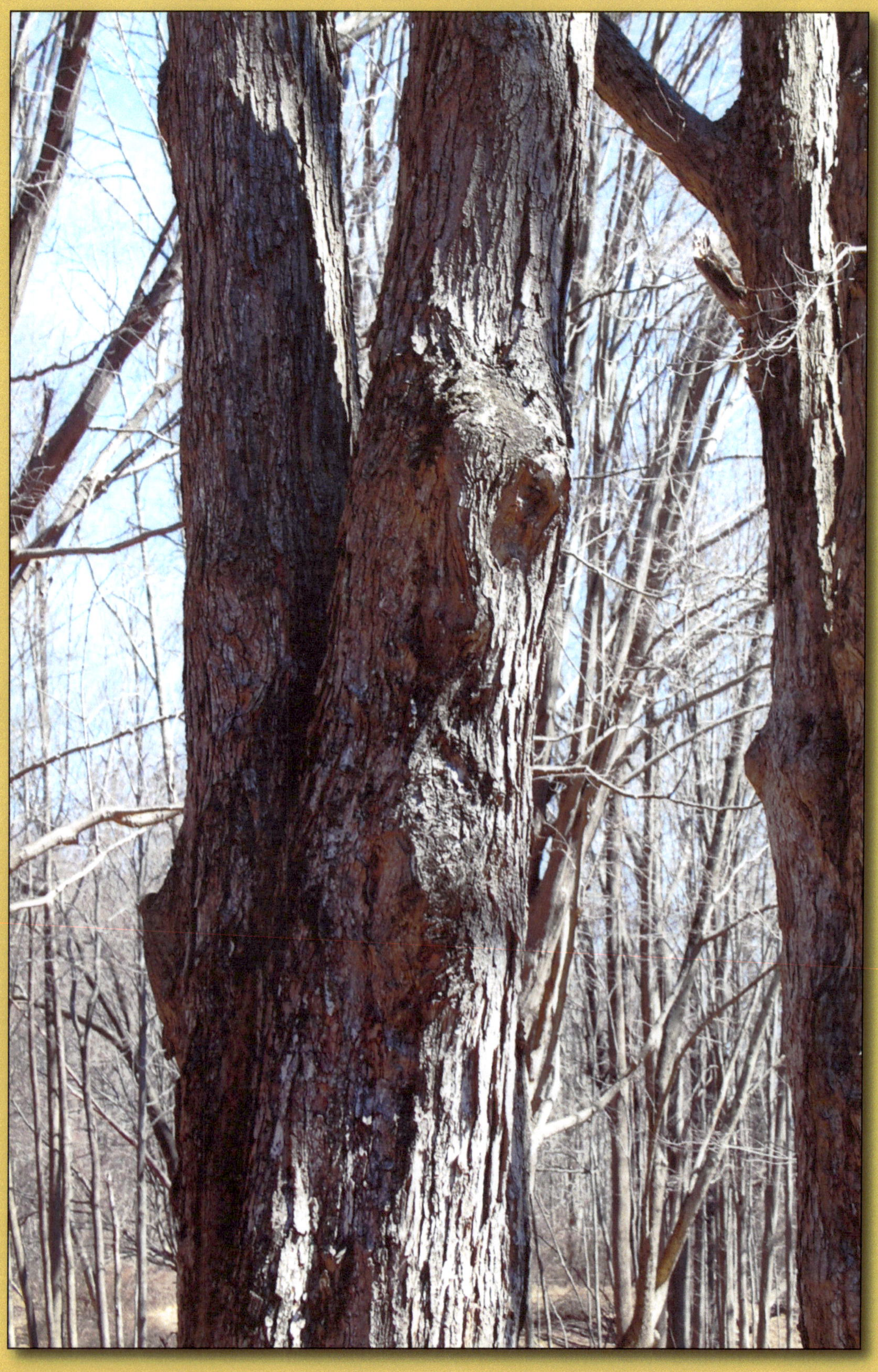

If one way be better than another, that you may be sure is Nature's way.

—*Aristotle, Nichomachean Ethics*

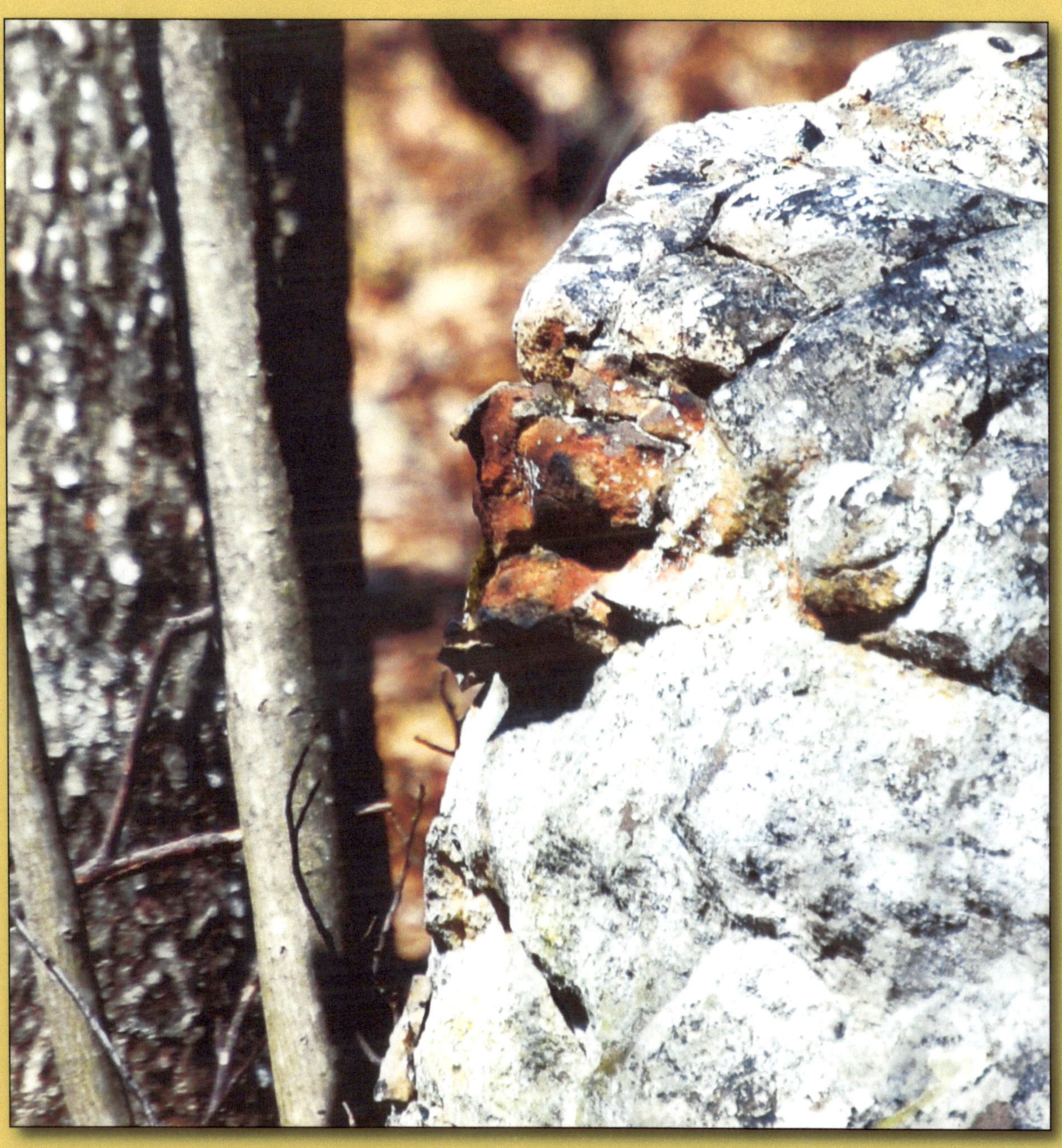

Adopt the pace of nature: her secret is patience.

—Ralph Waldo Emerson

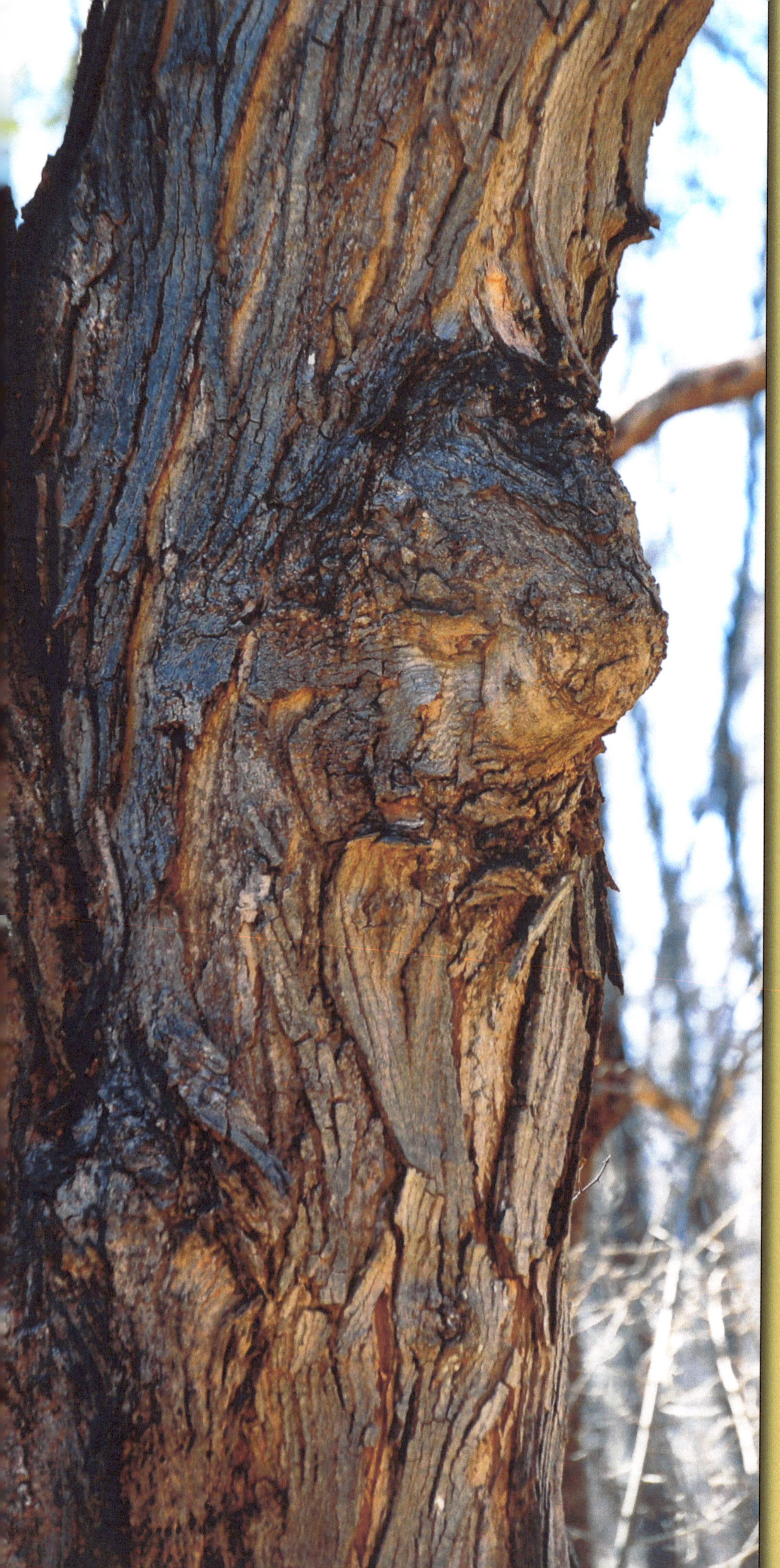

The mind, in proportion as it is cut off from free communication with nature, with revelation, with God, with itself, loses its life, just as the body droops when debarred from the air and the cheering light from heaven.

—*William Channing*

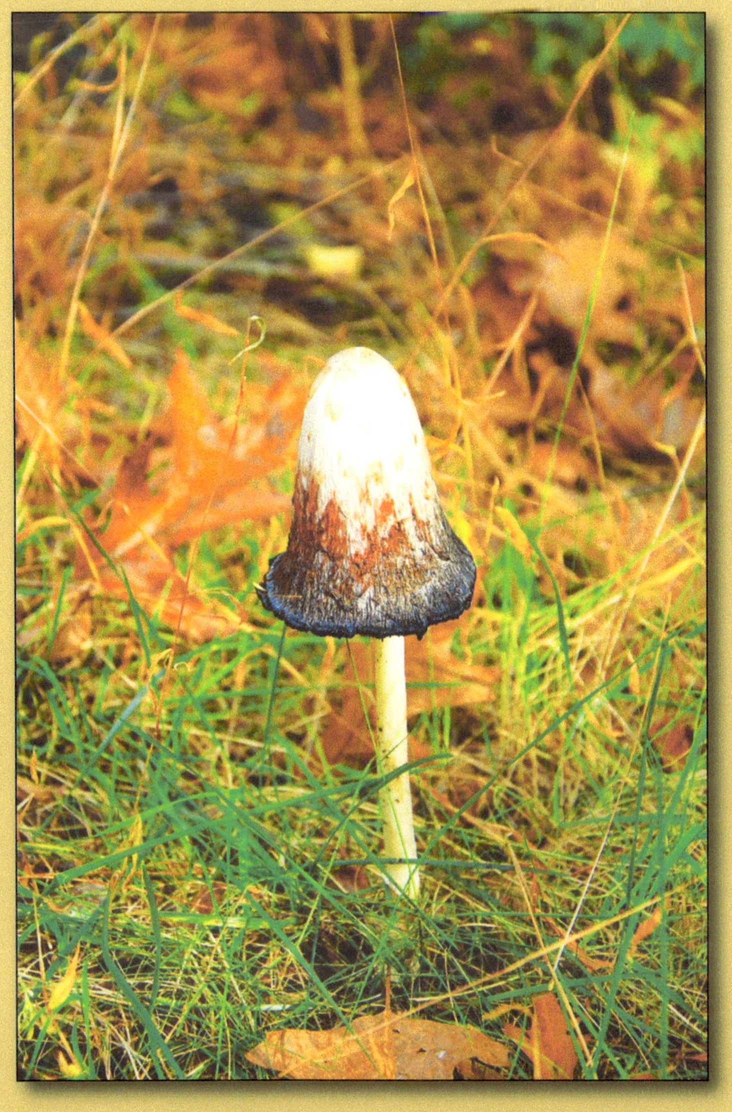

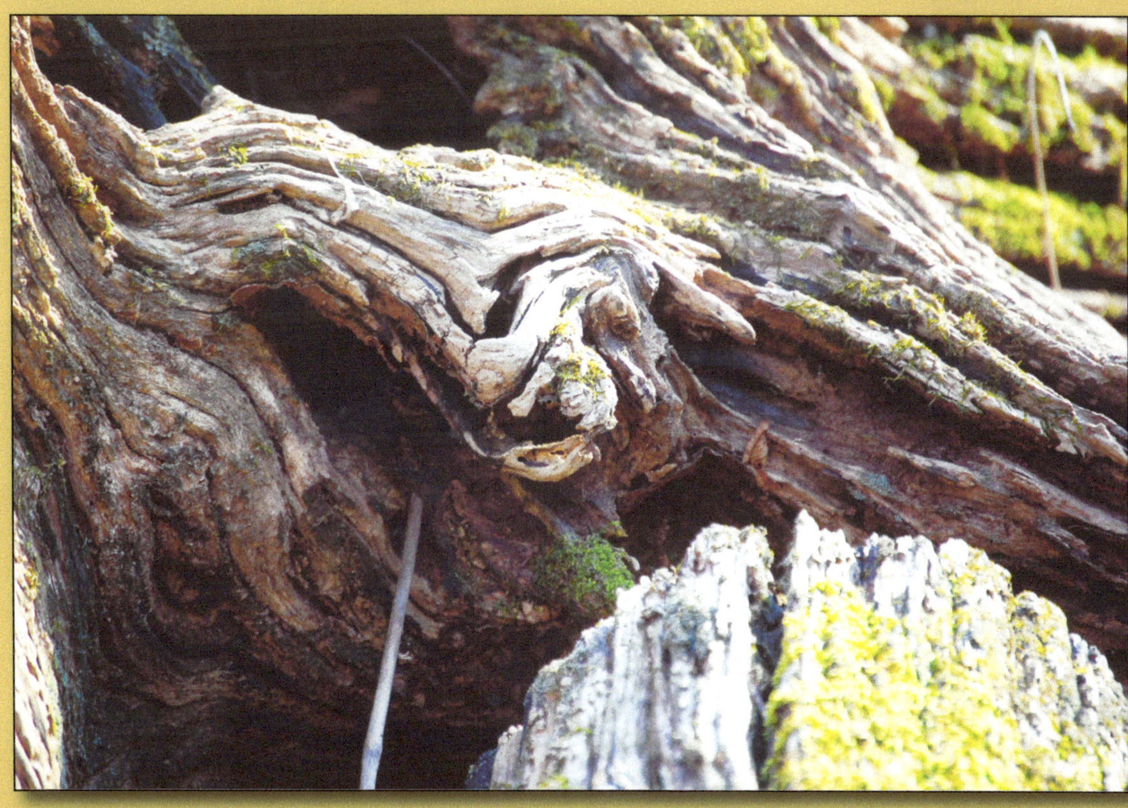

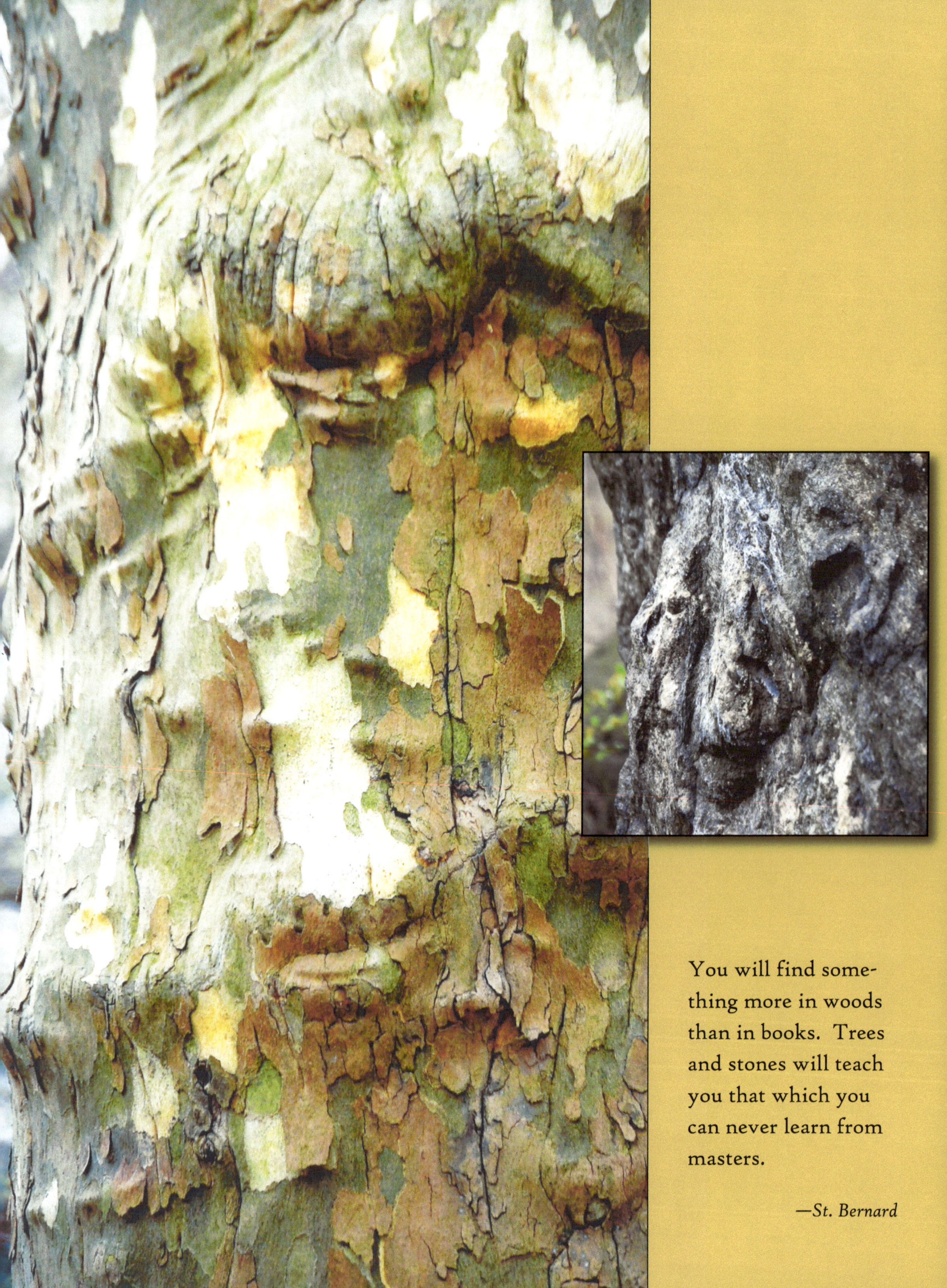

You will find something more in woods than in books. Trees and stones will teach you that which you can never learn from masters.

—St. Bernard

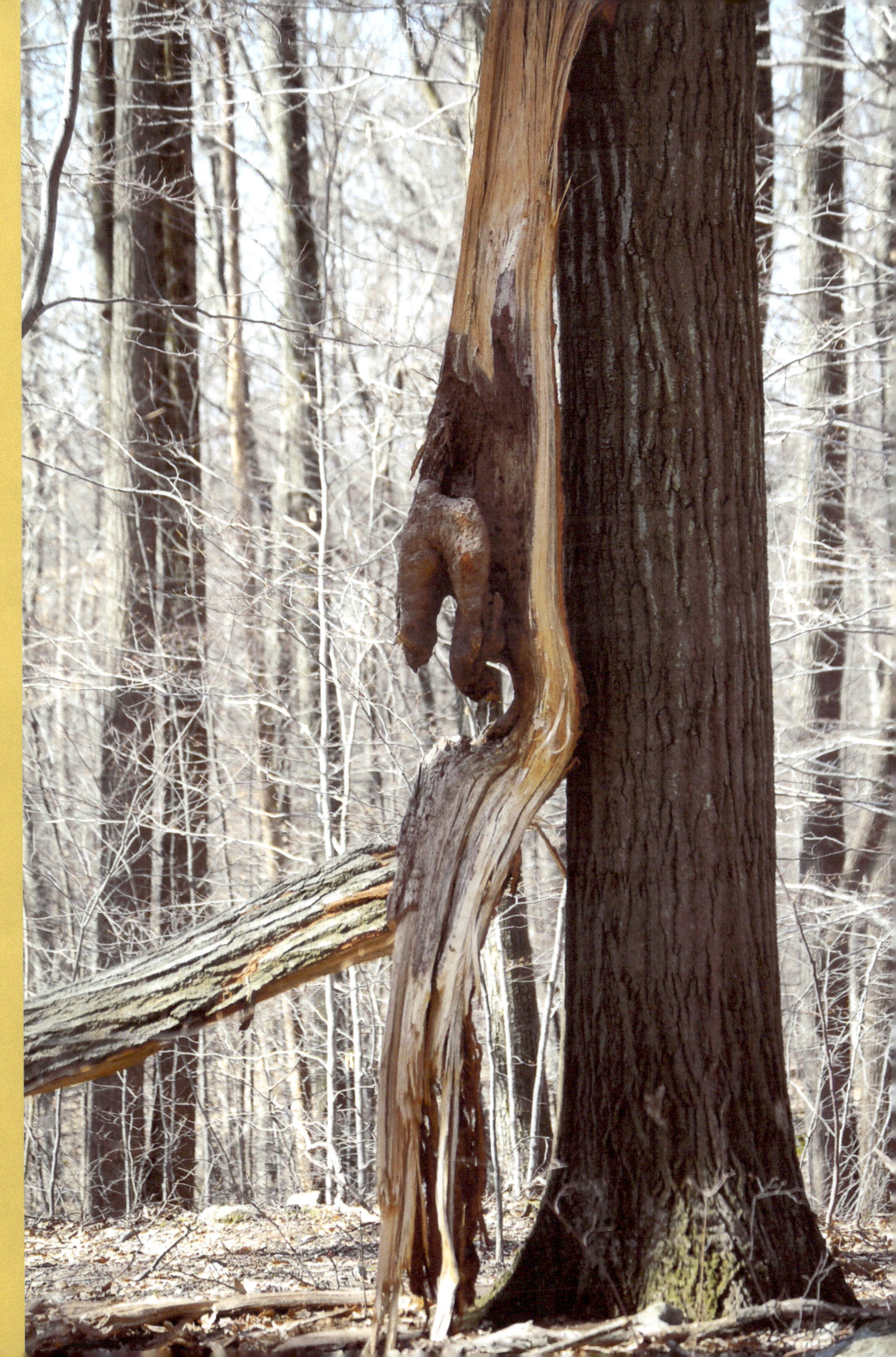

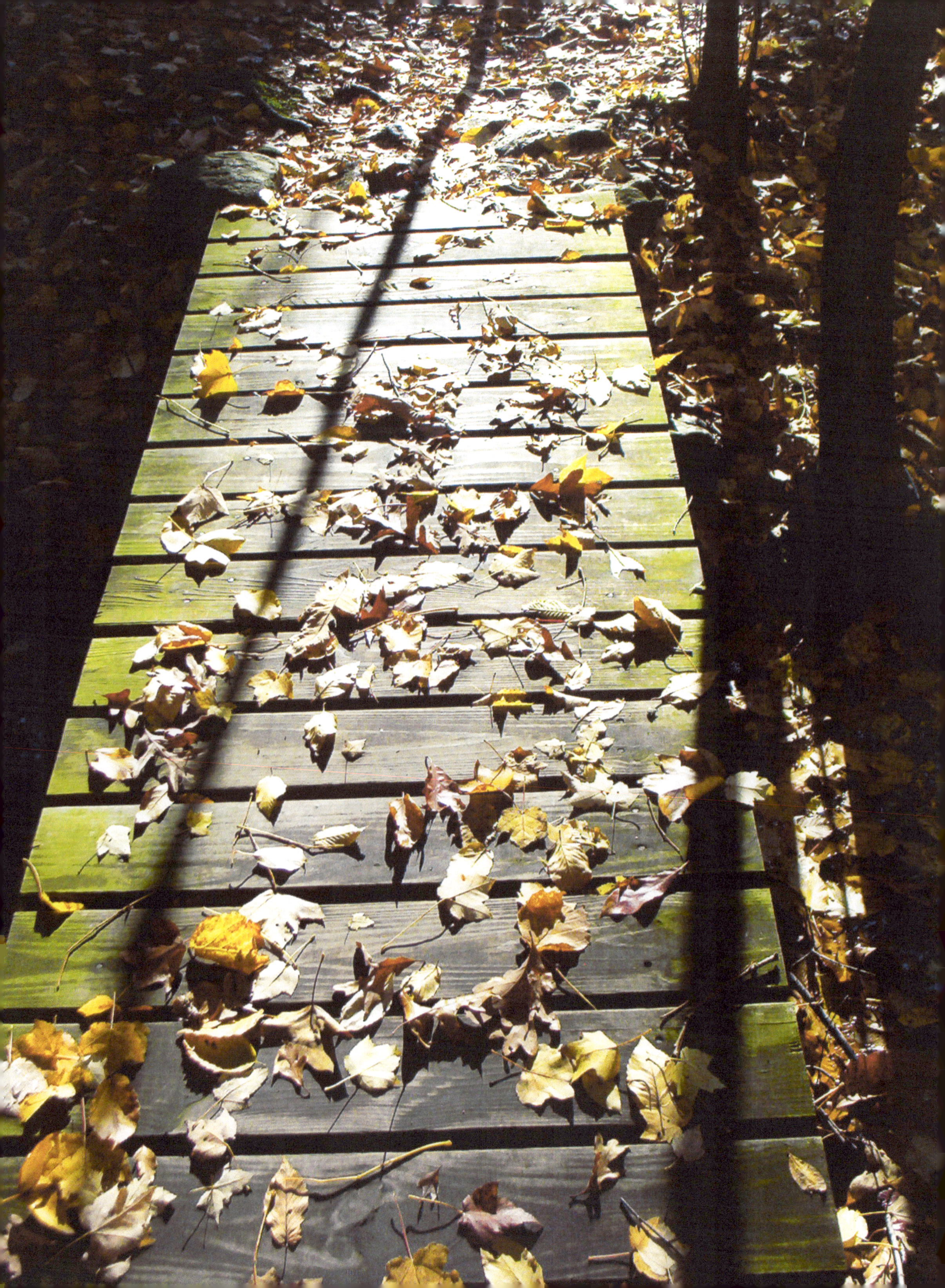

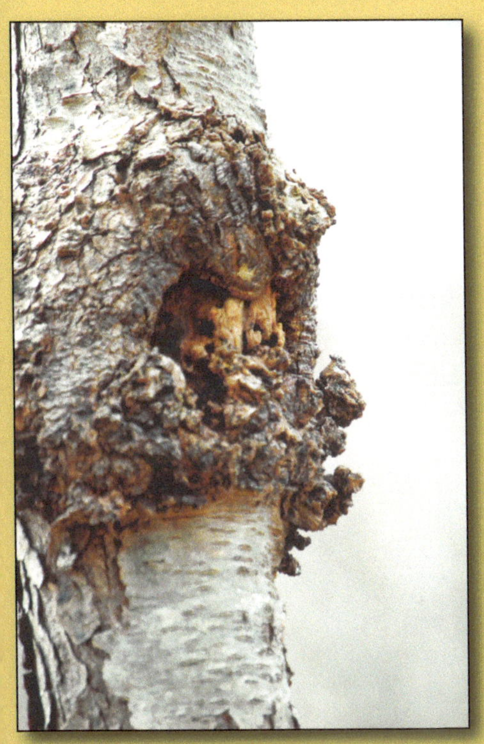

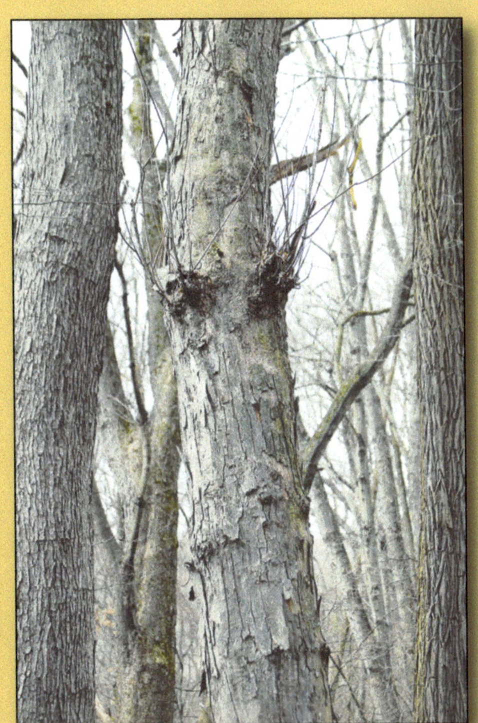

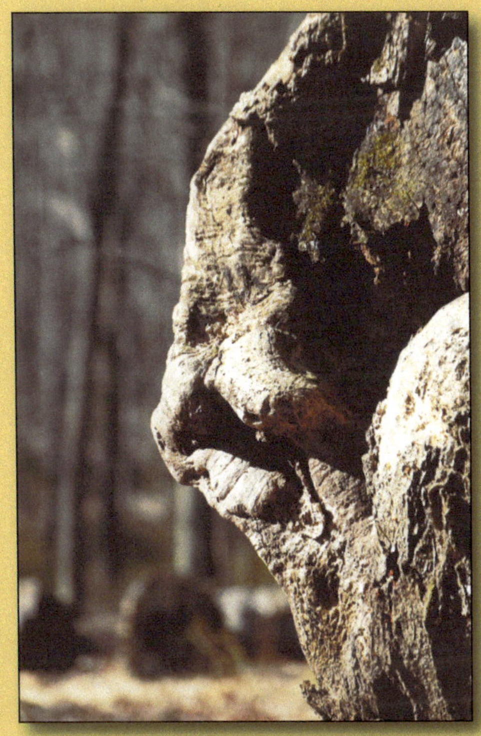

If a man walks in the woods for love of them half of each day, he is in danger of being regarded as a loafer. But if he spends his days as a speculator, shearing off those woods and making the earth bald before her time, he is deemed an industrious and enterprising citizen.

—*Henry David Thoreau*

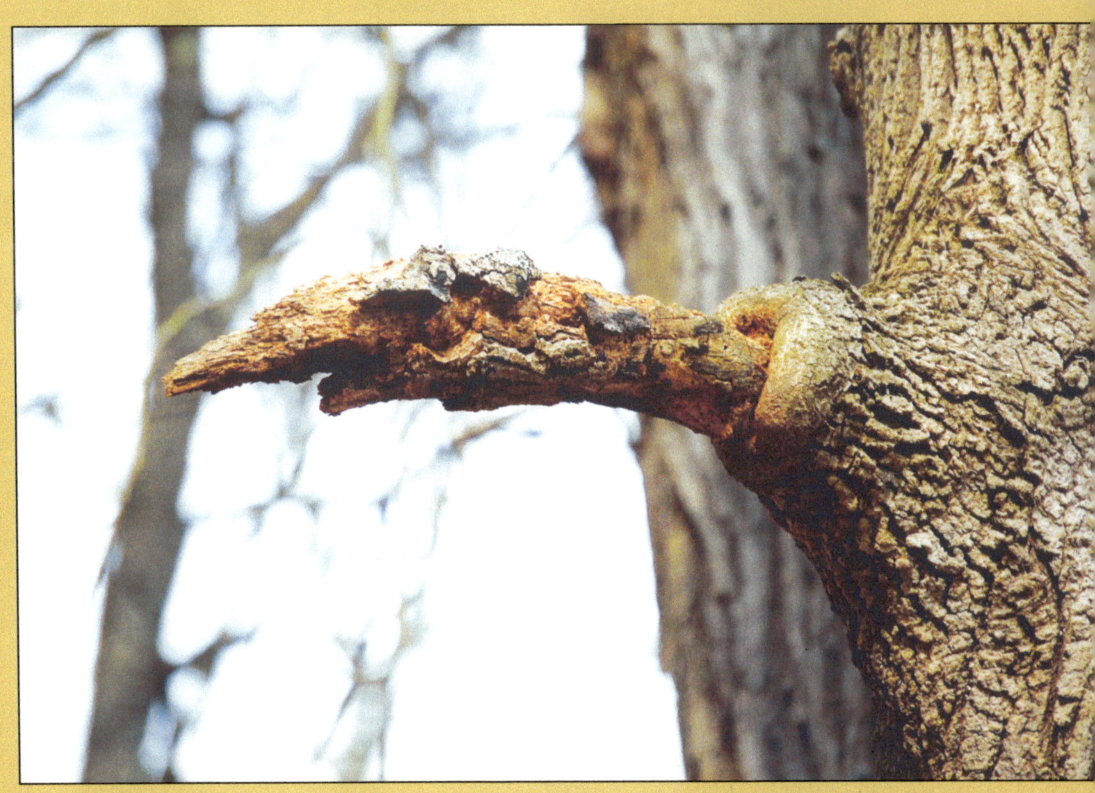

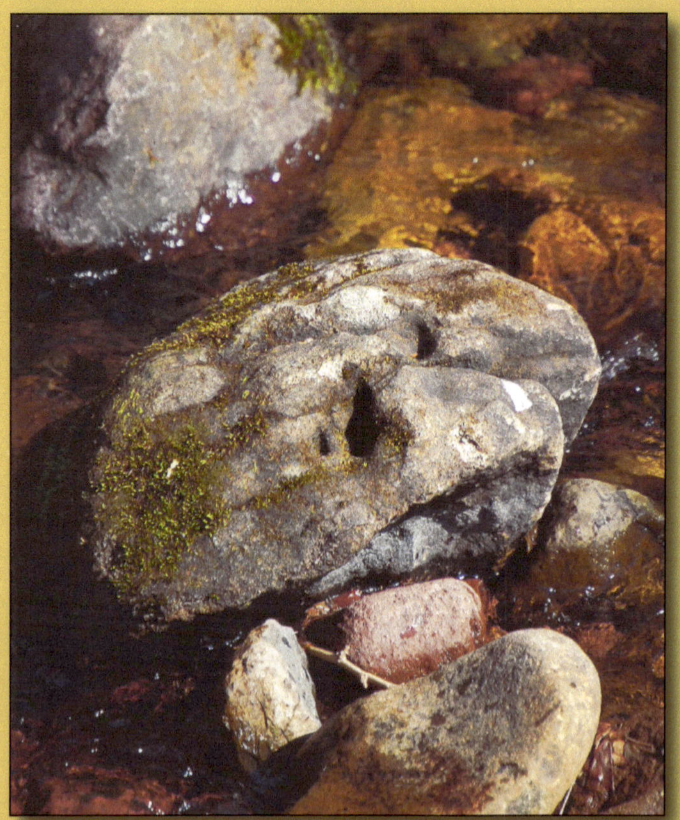

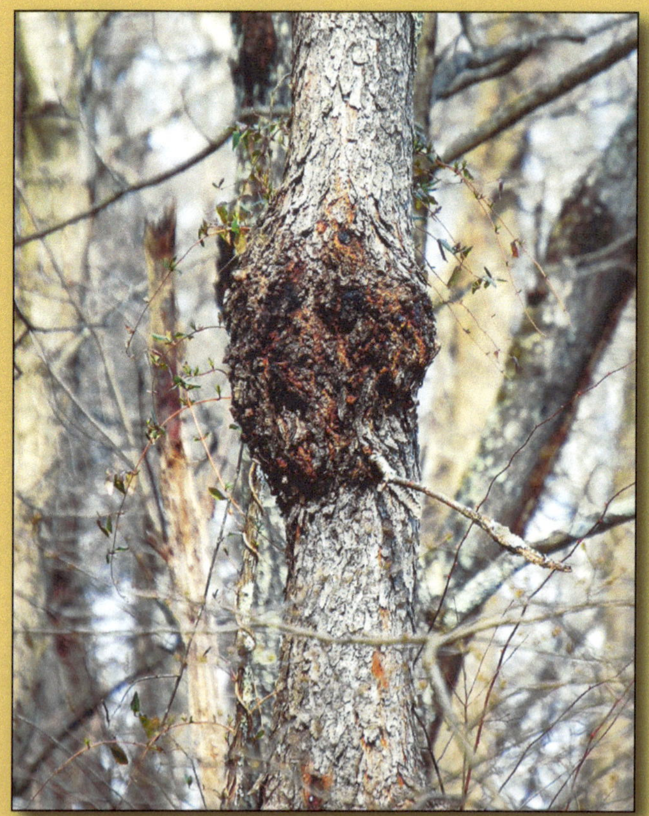

I love to think of nature as an unlimited broadcasting station, through which God speaks to us every hour, if we will only tune in.

—George Washington Carver

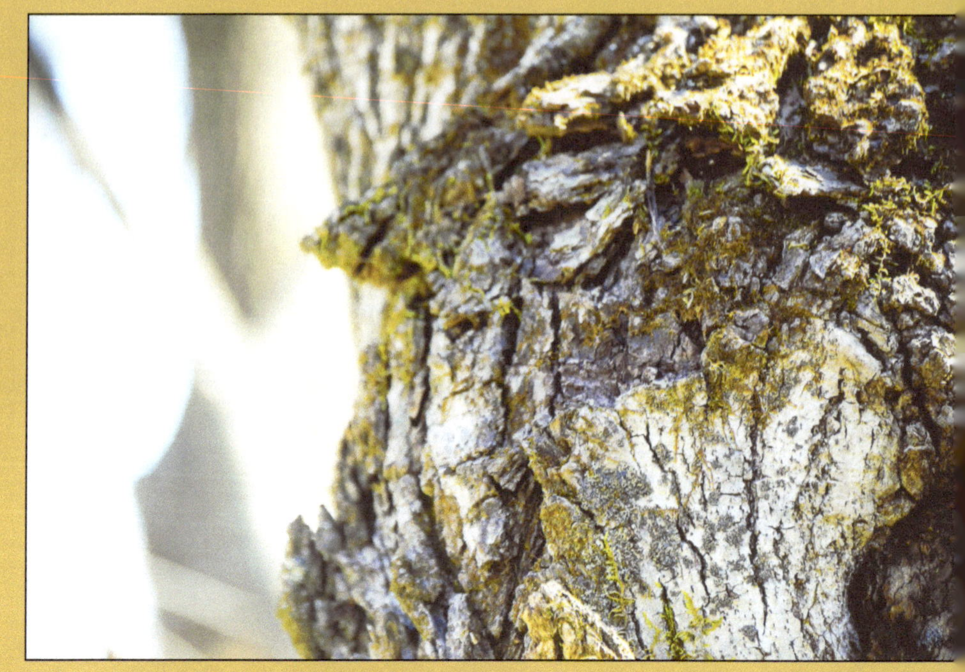

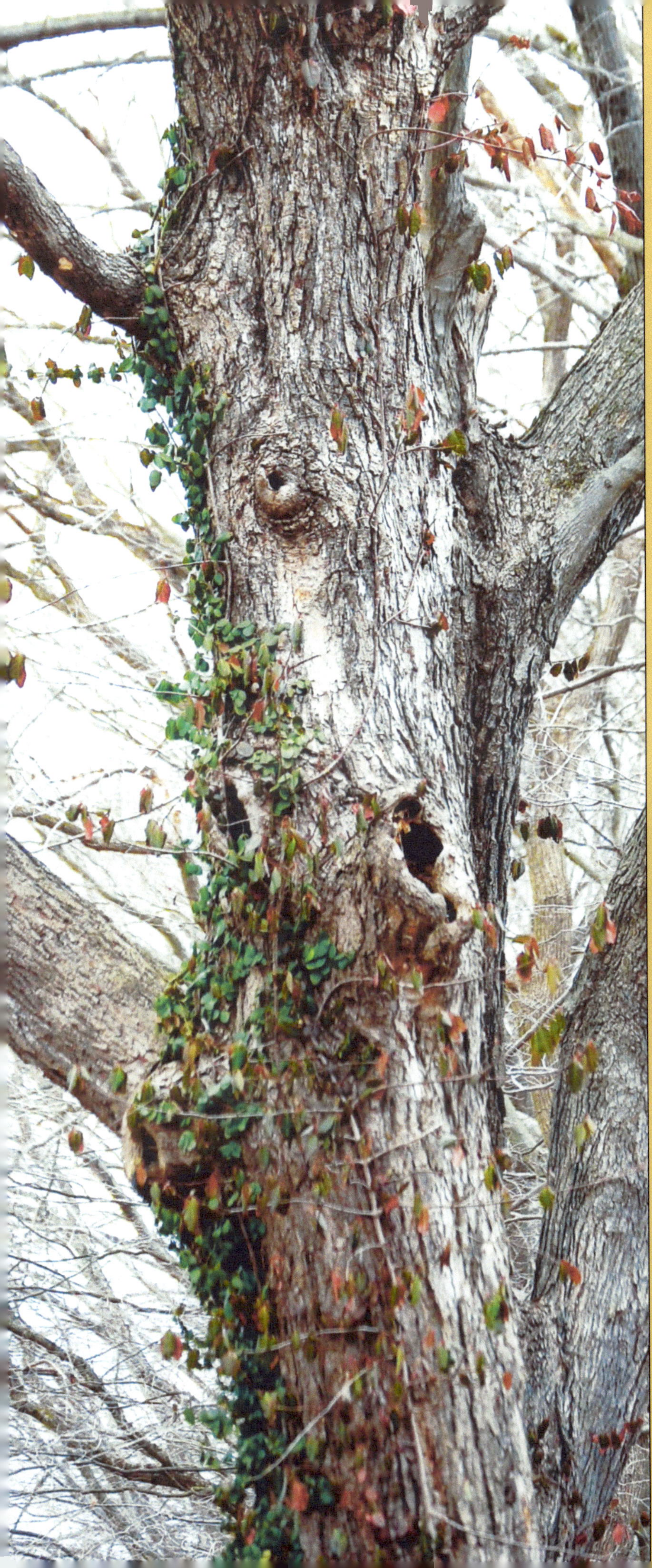

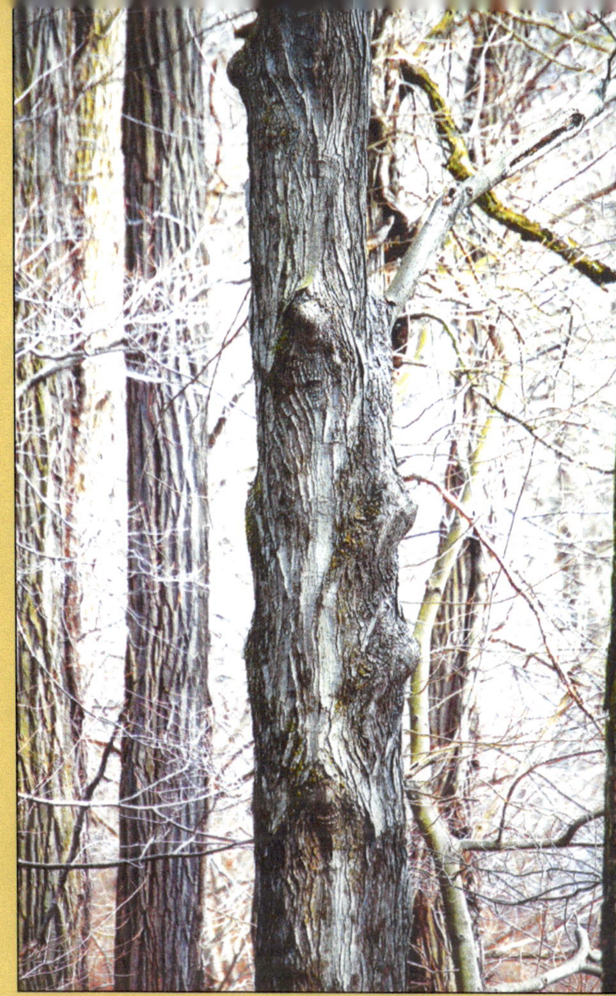

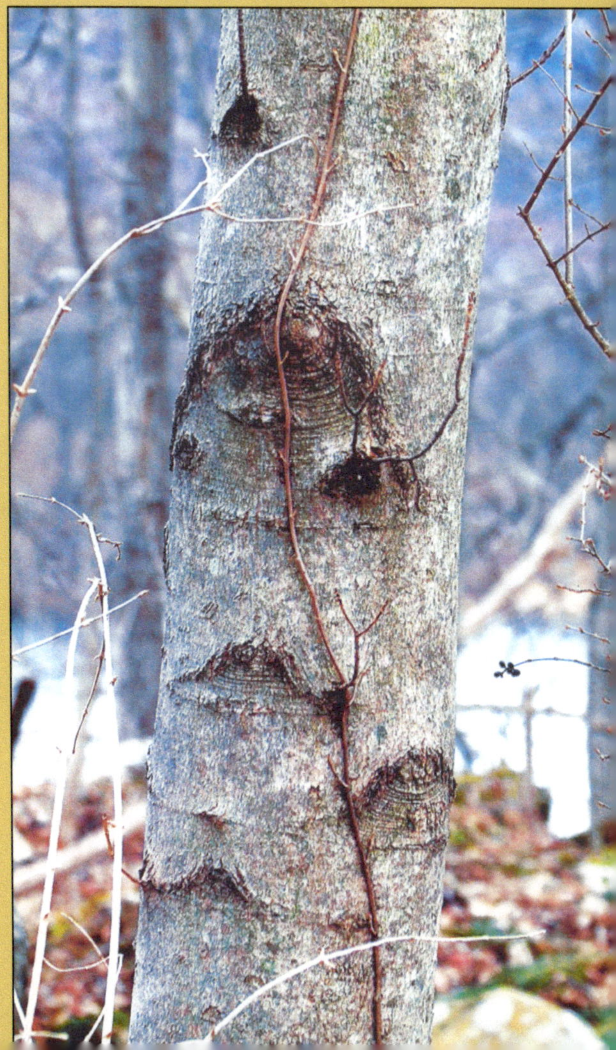

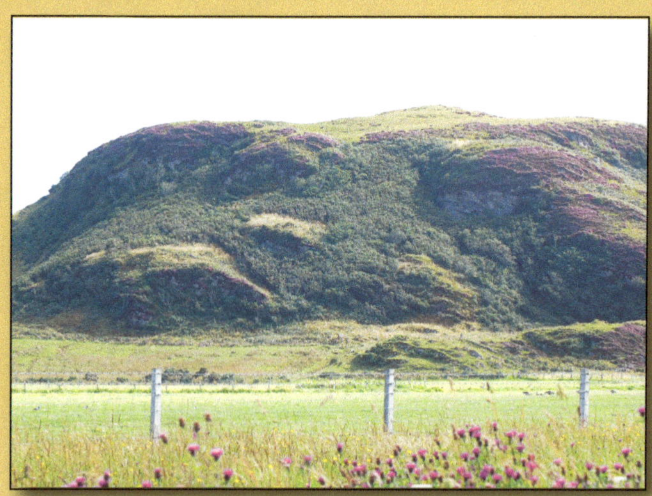

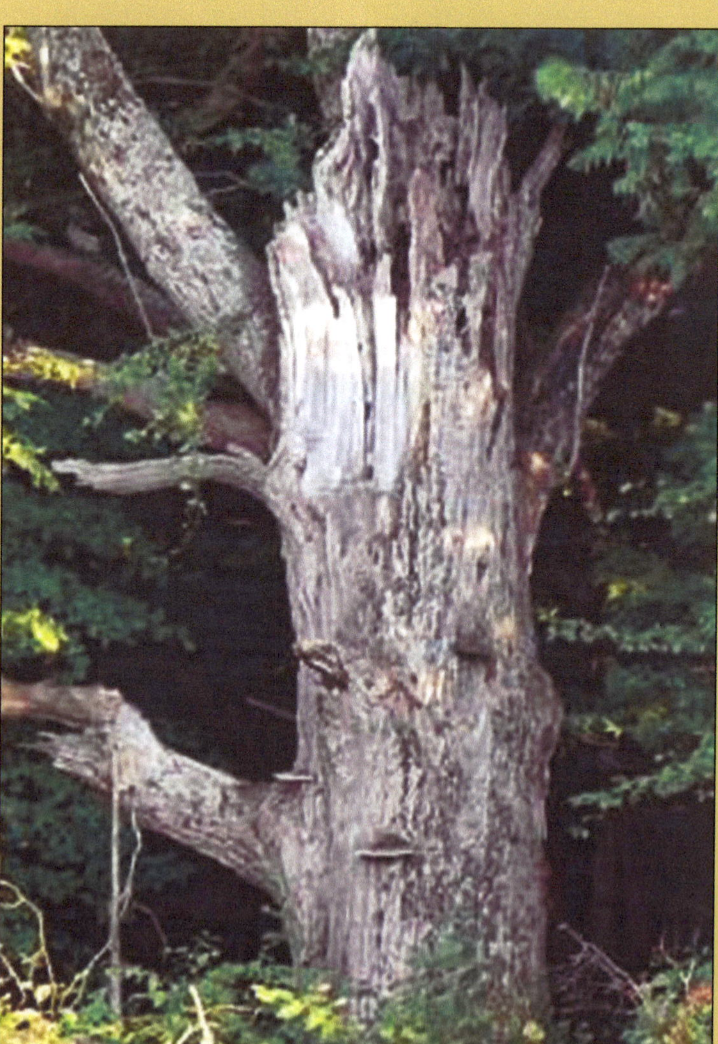

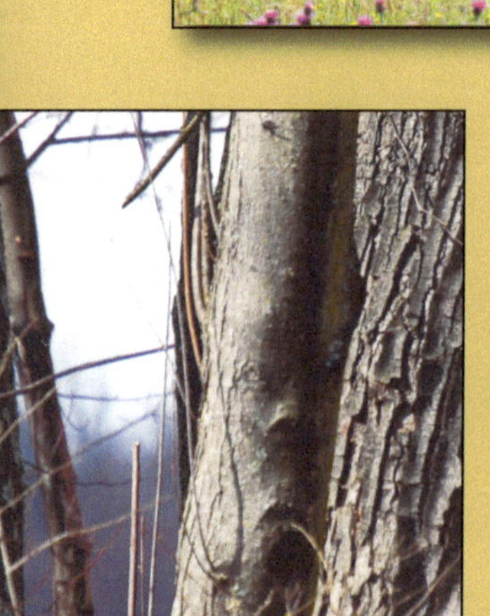

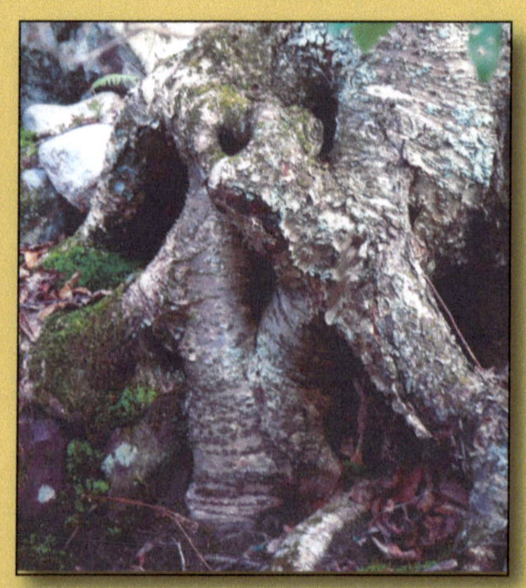

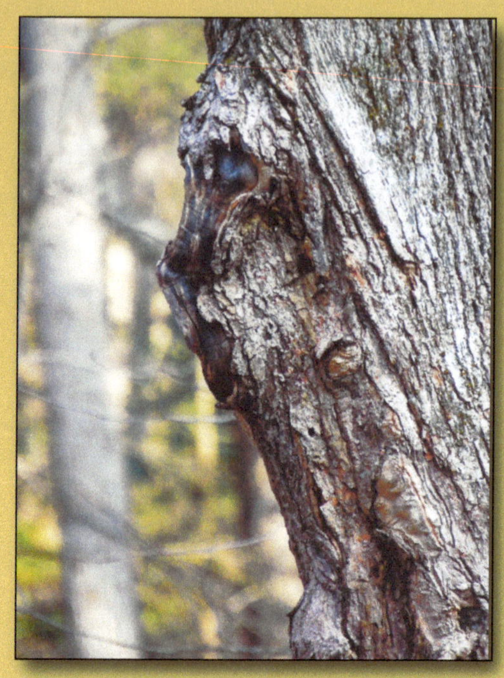

It is not so much for its beauty that the forest makes a claim upon men's hearts, as for that subtle something, that quality of air that emanation from old trees, that so wonderfully changes and renews a weary spirit.

—Robert Louis Stevenson

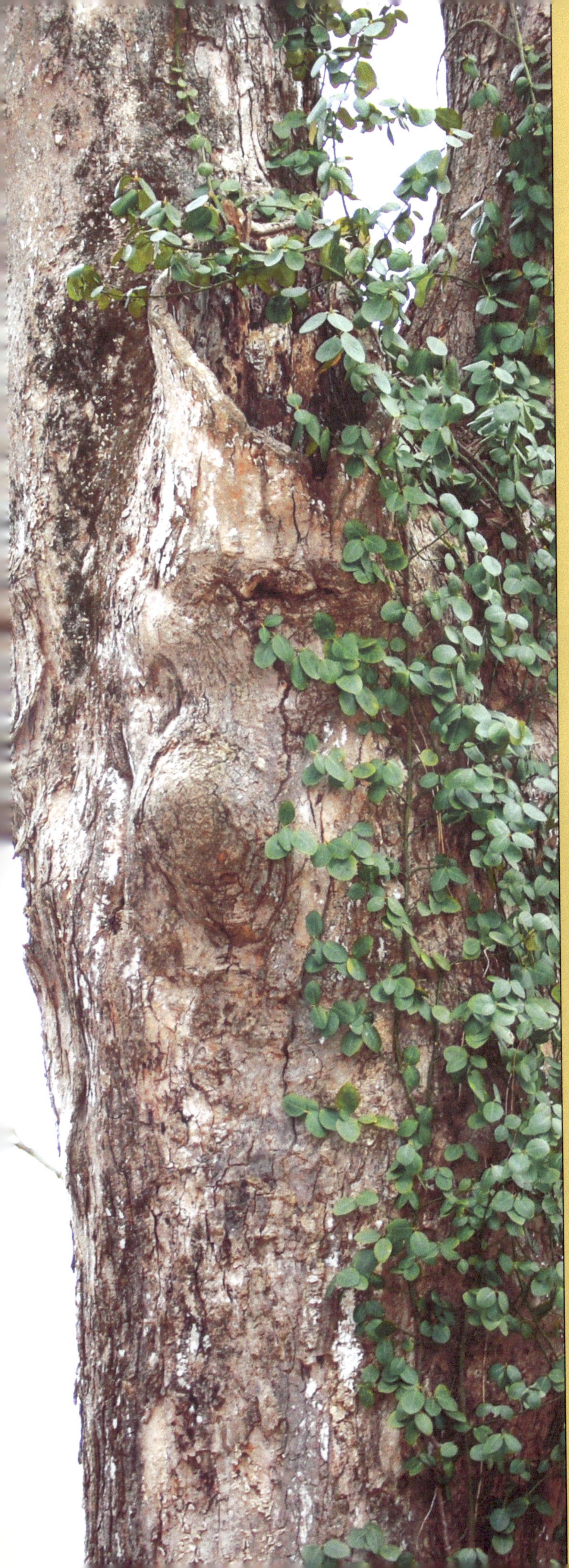

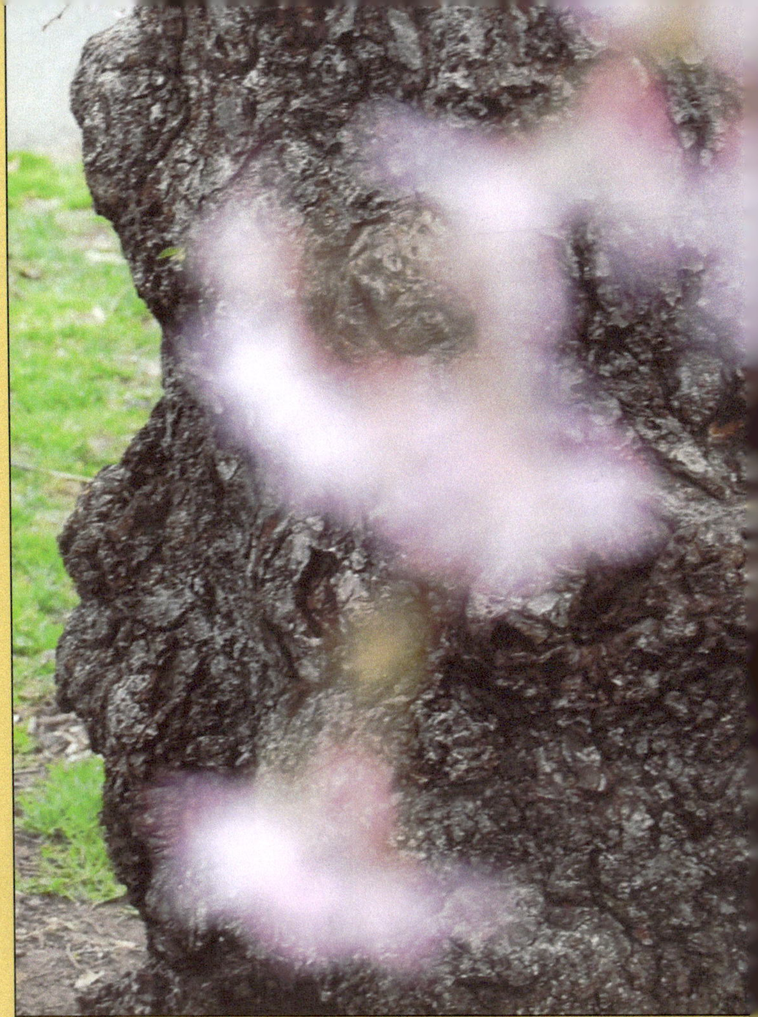

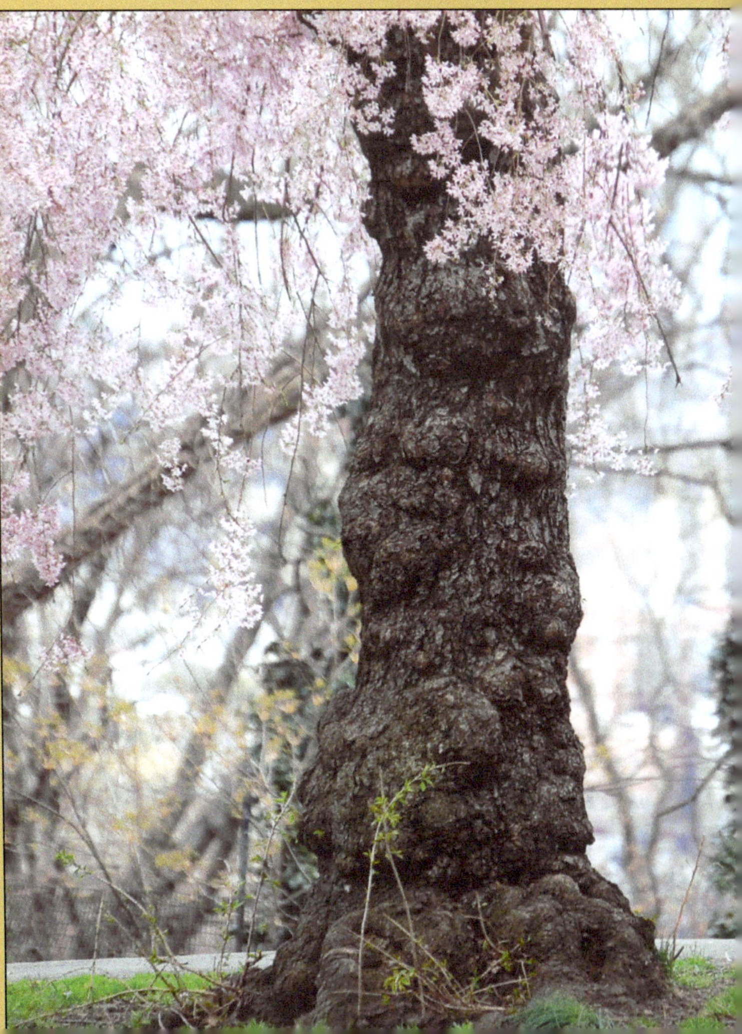

The oaks and the pines, and their brethren of the wood, have seen so many suns rise and set, so many seasons come and go, and so many generations pass into silence, that we may well wonder what "the story of the trees" would be to us if they had tongues to tell it, or we ears fine enough to understand.

—*Anon., quoted in "Quotations for Special Occasions," by Maud van Buren, 1938*

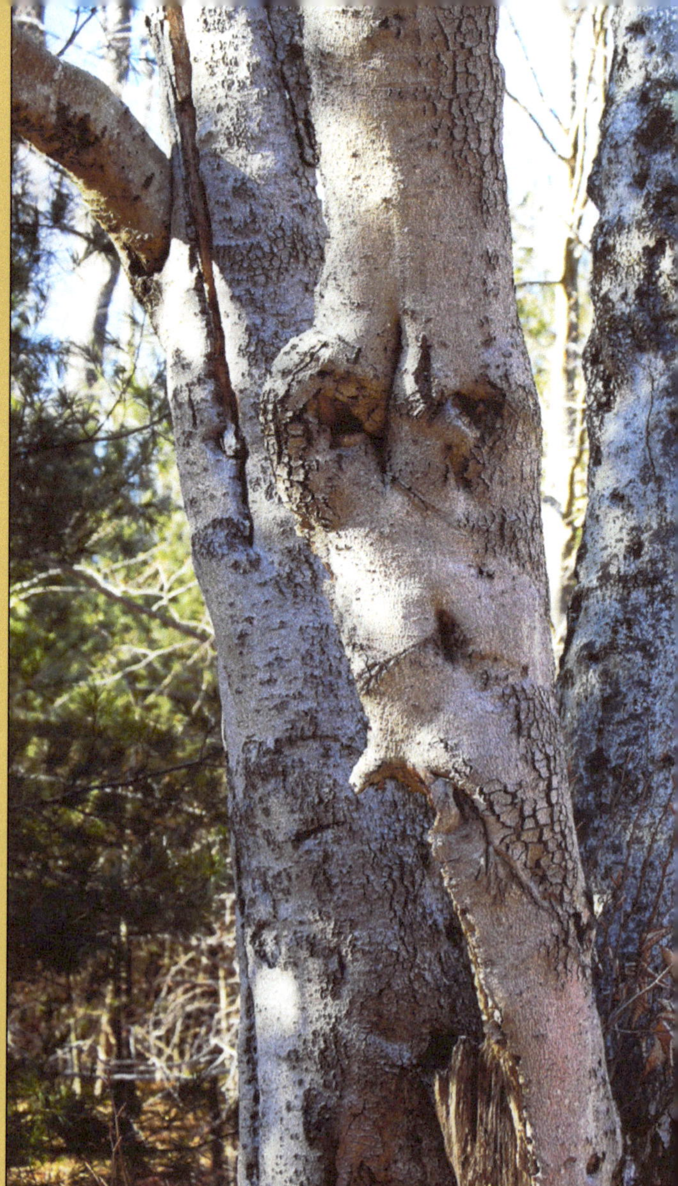

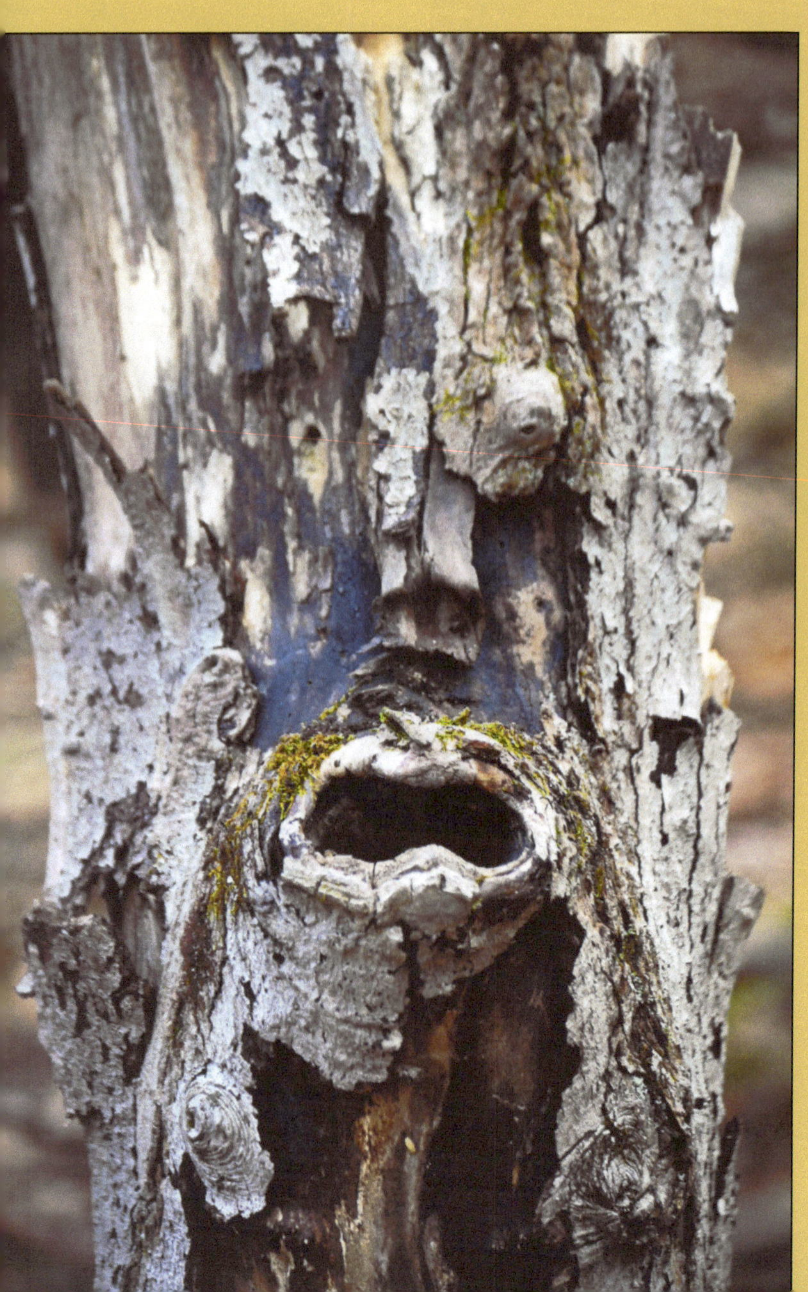

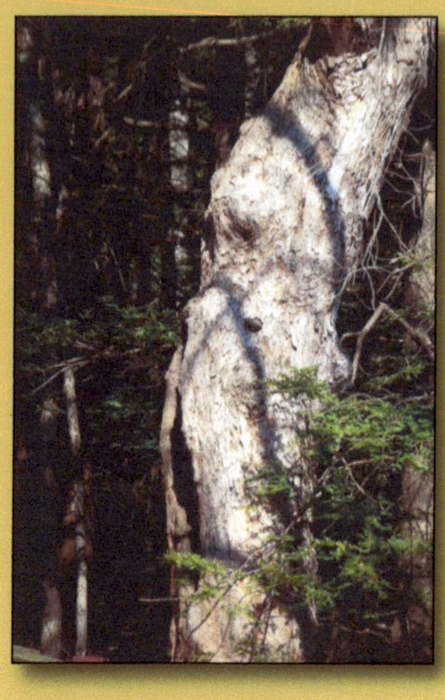

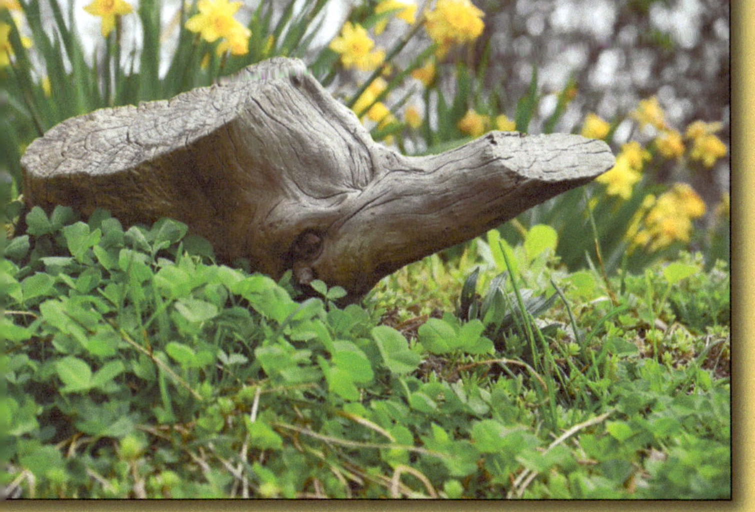

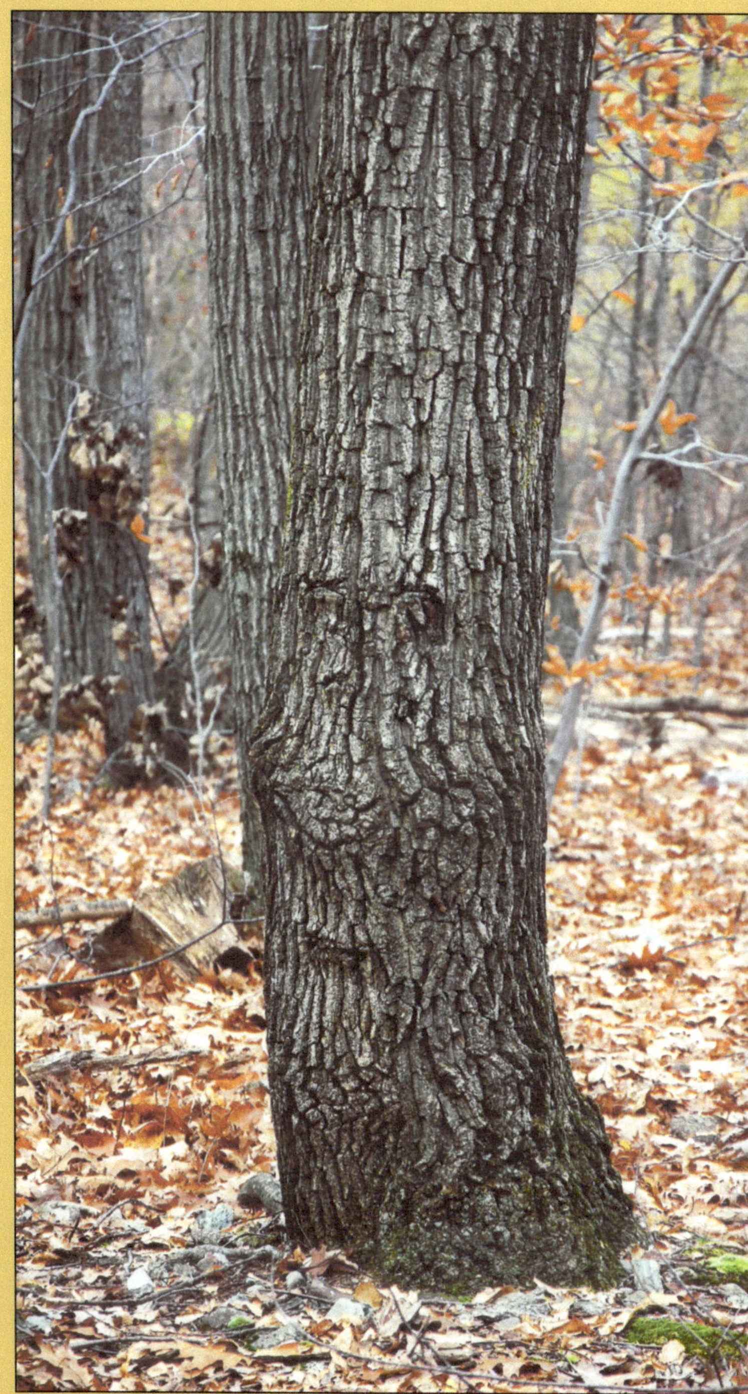

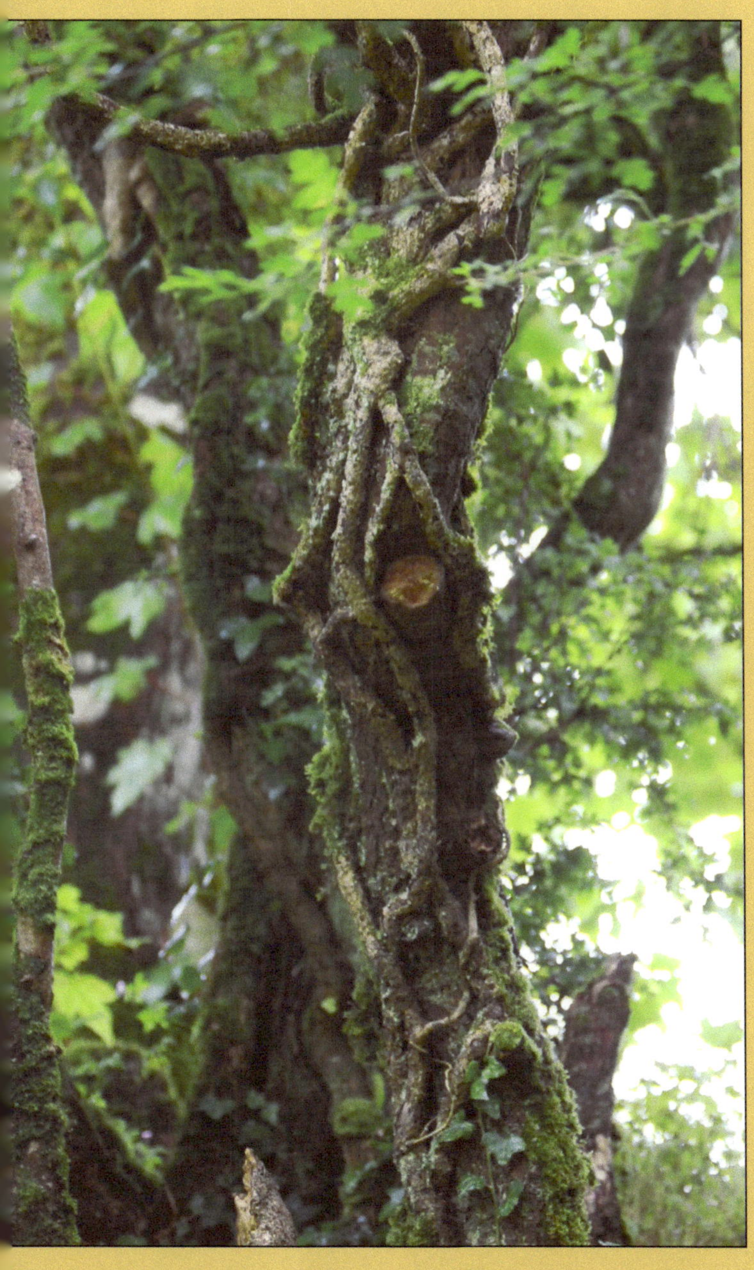

The life of nature we must meet halfway; it is shy, withdrawn, and blends itself with a vast neutral background. We must be initiated; it is an order the secrets of which are well guarded.

—John Burroughs

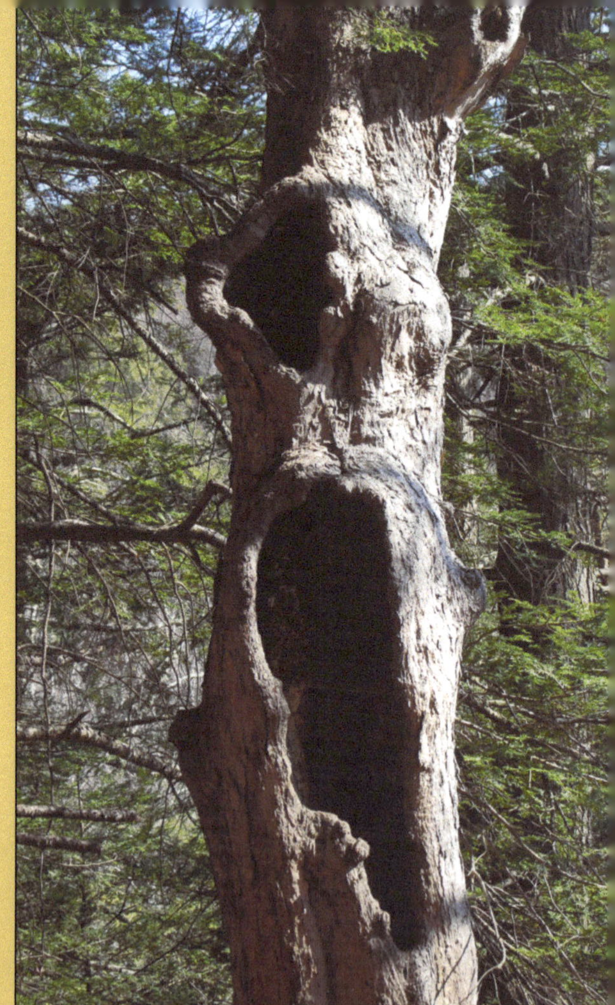

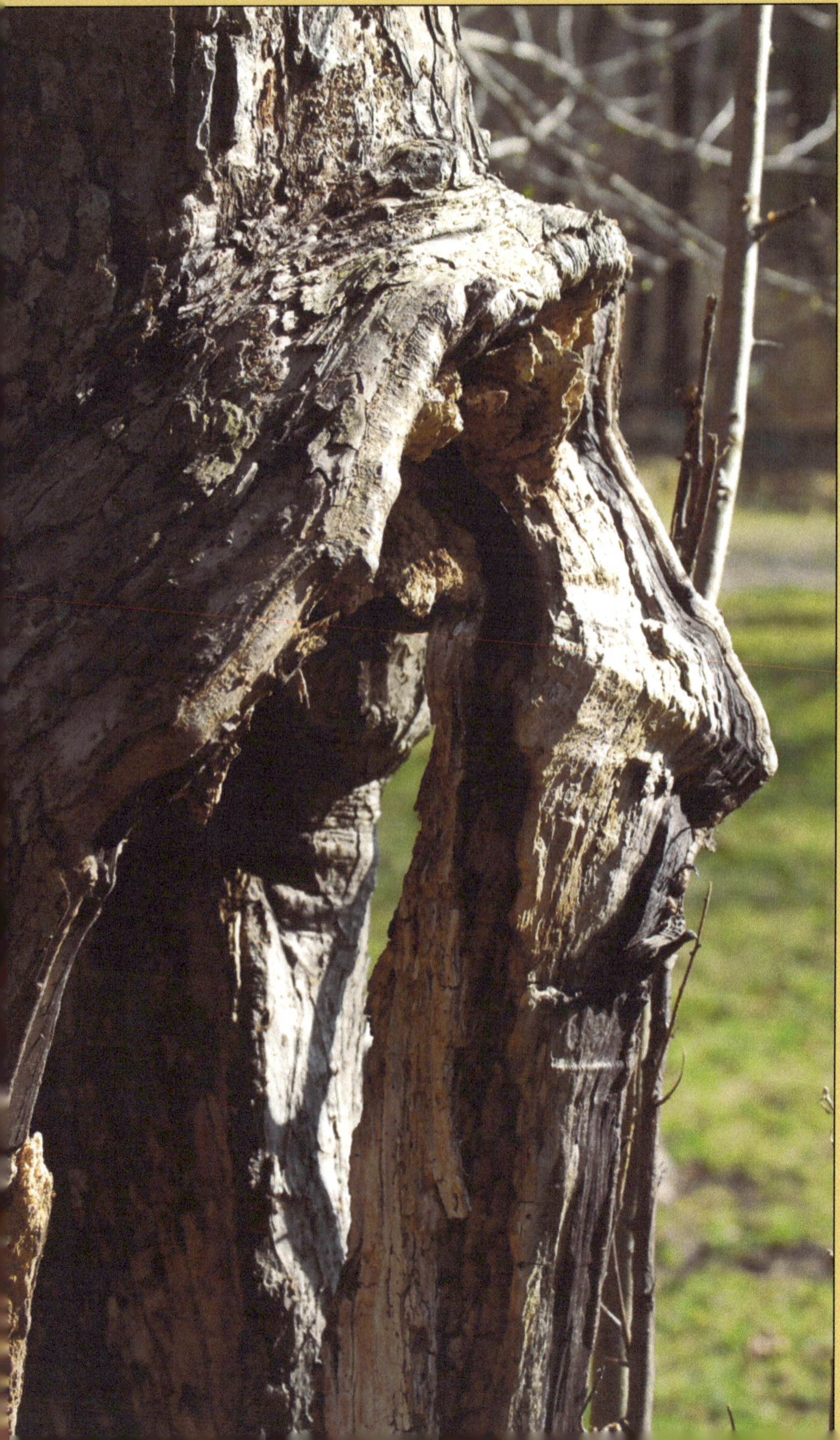

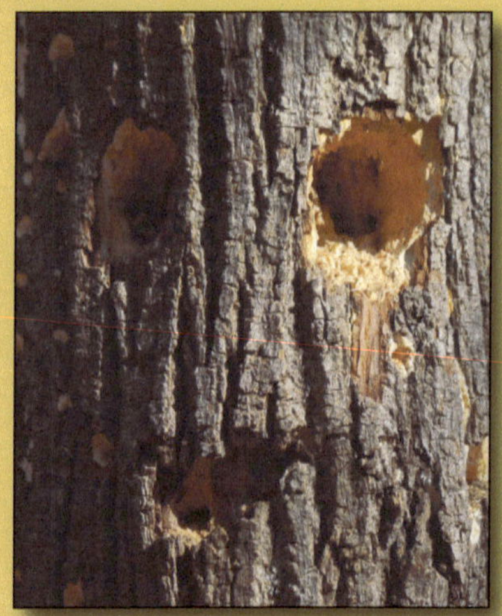

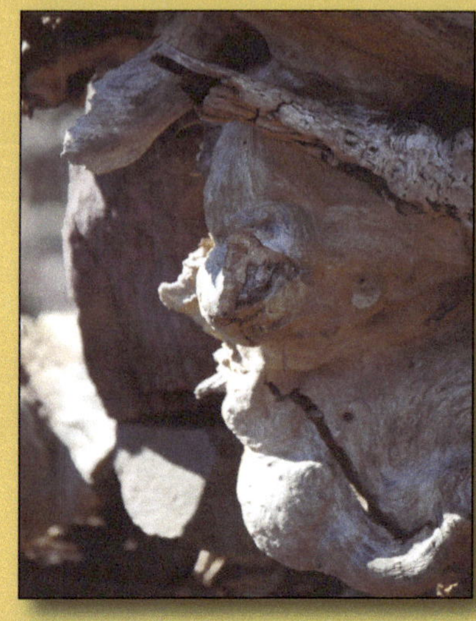

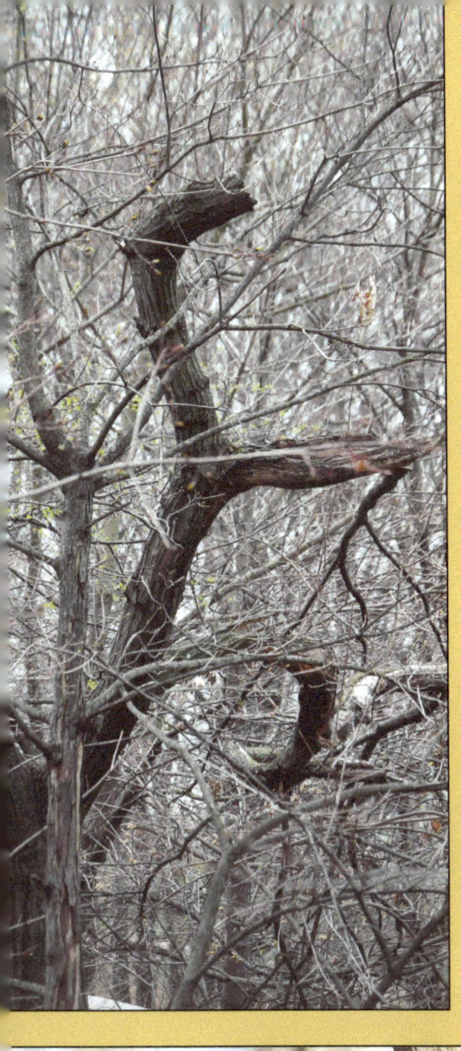
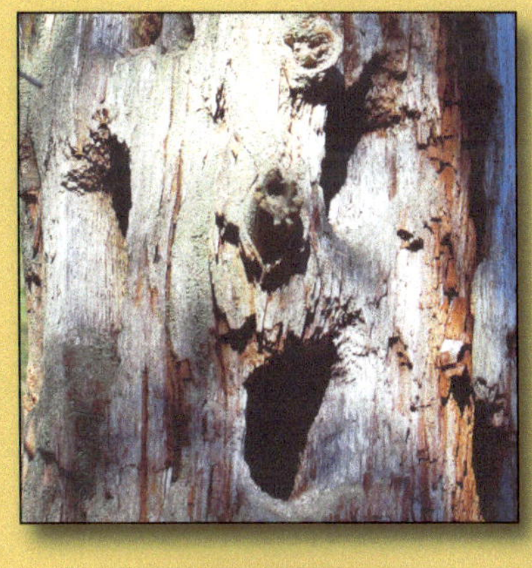
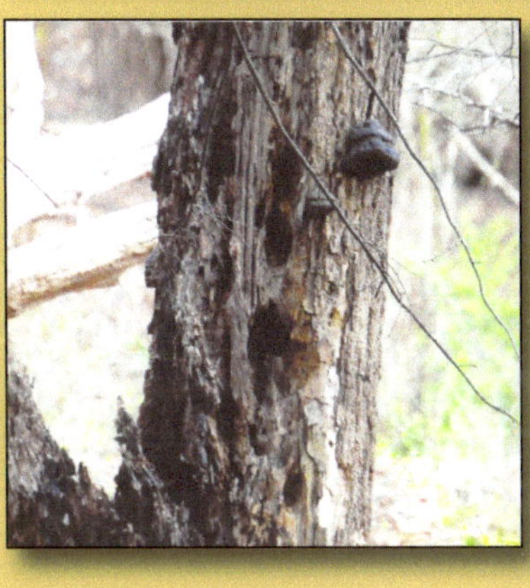
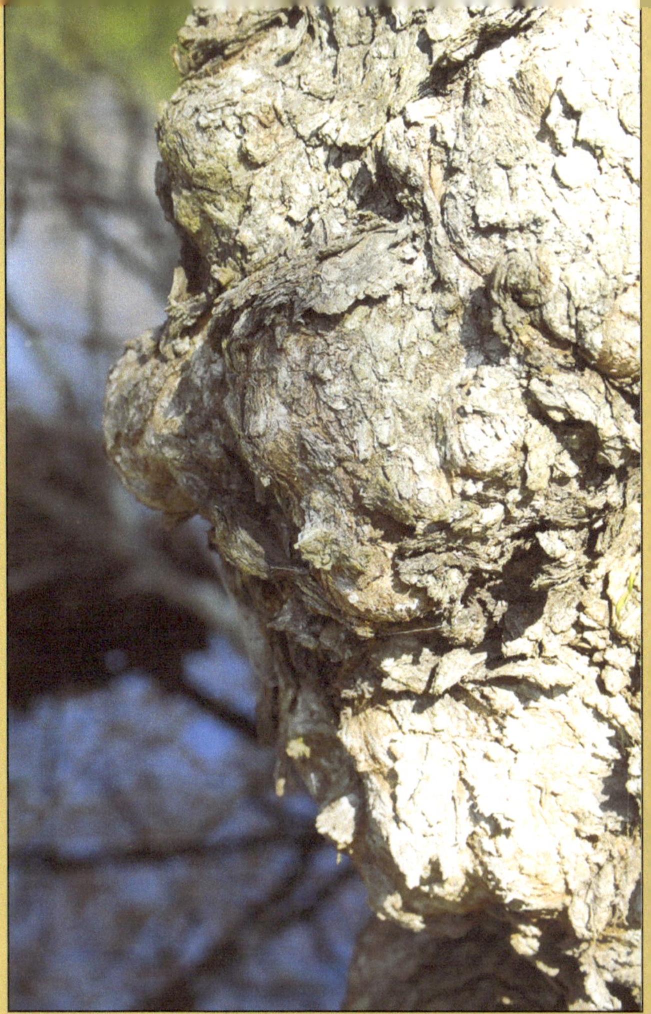
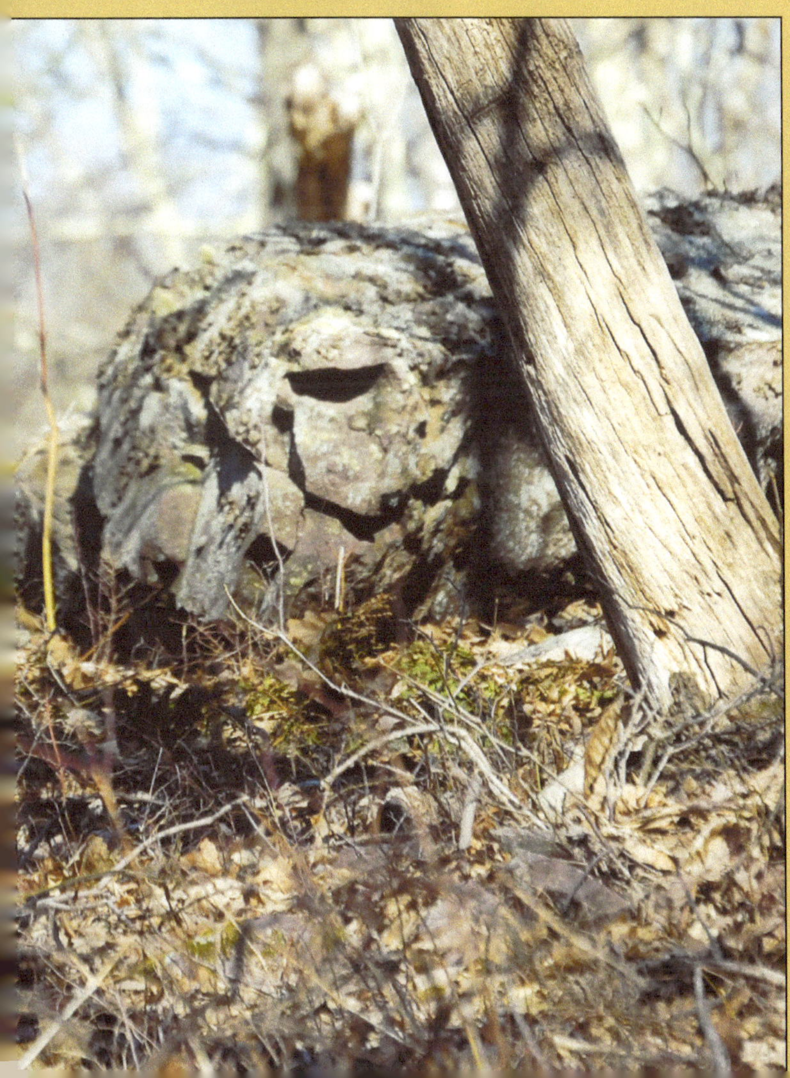
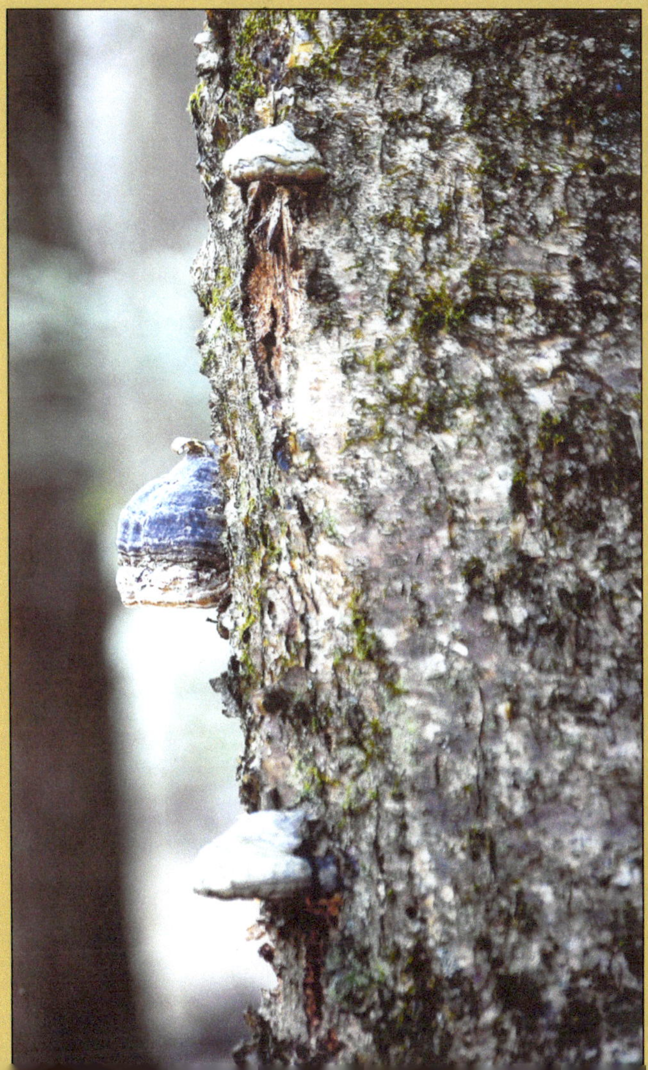

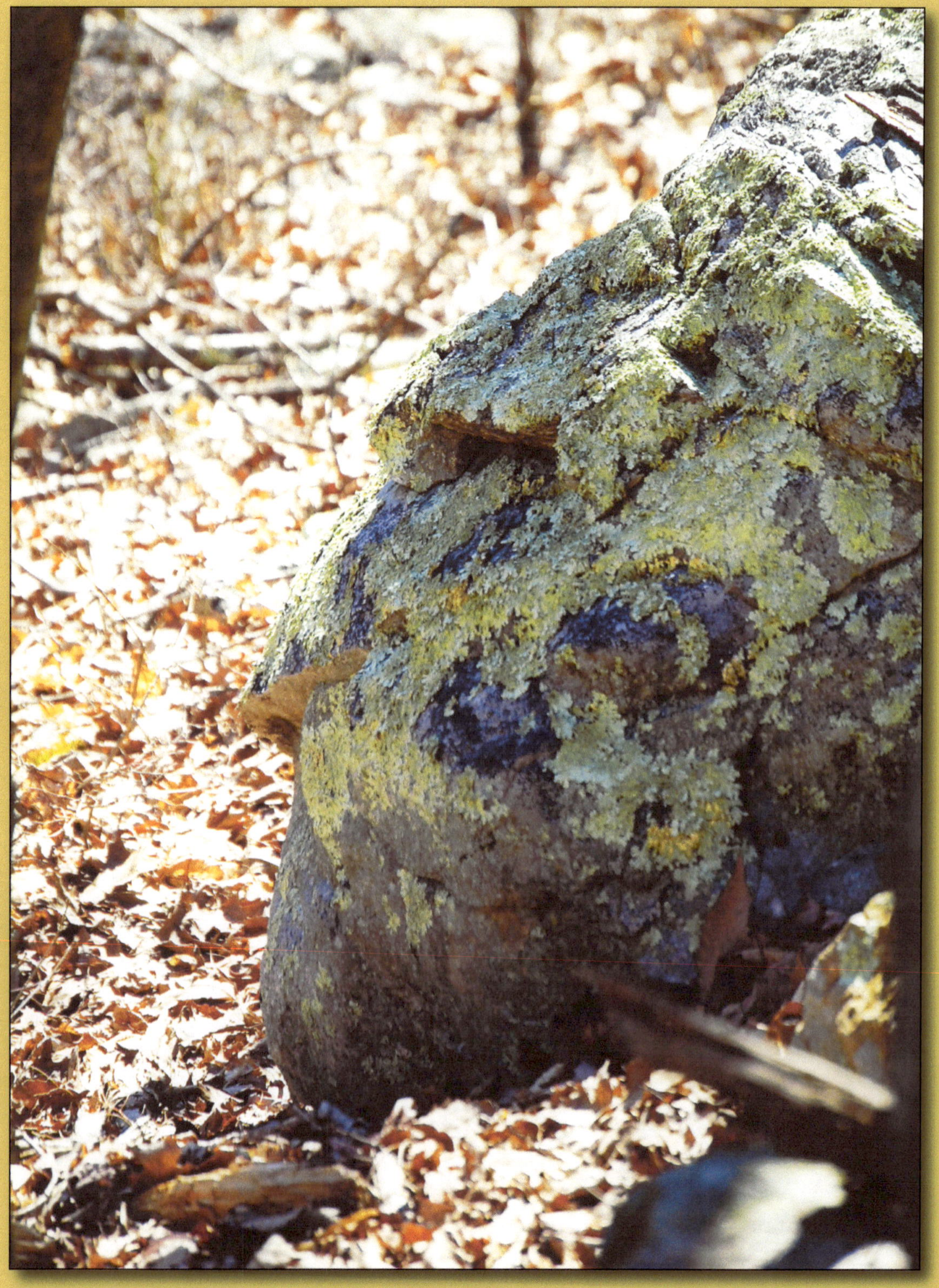

Nature teaches more than she preaches. There are no sermons in stones. It is easier to get a spark out of a stone than a moral.

—John Burroughs

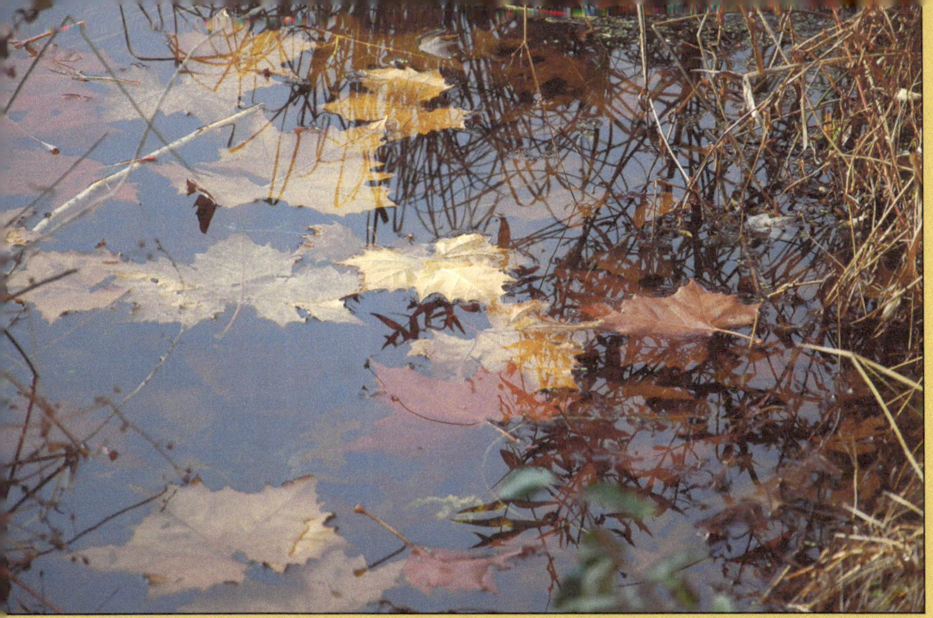

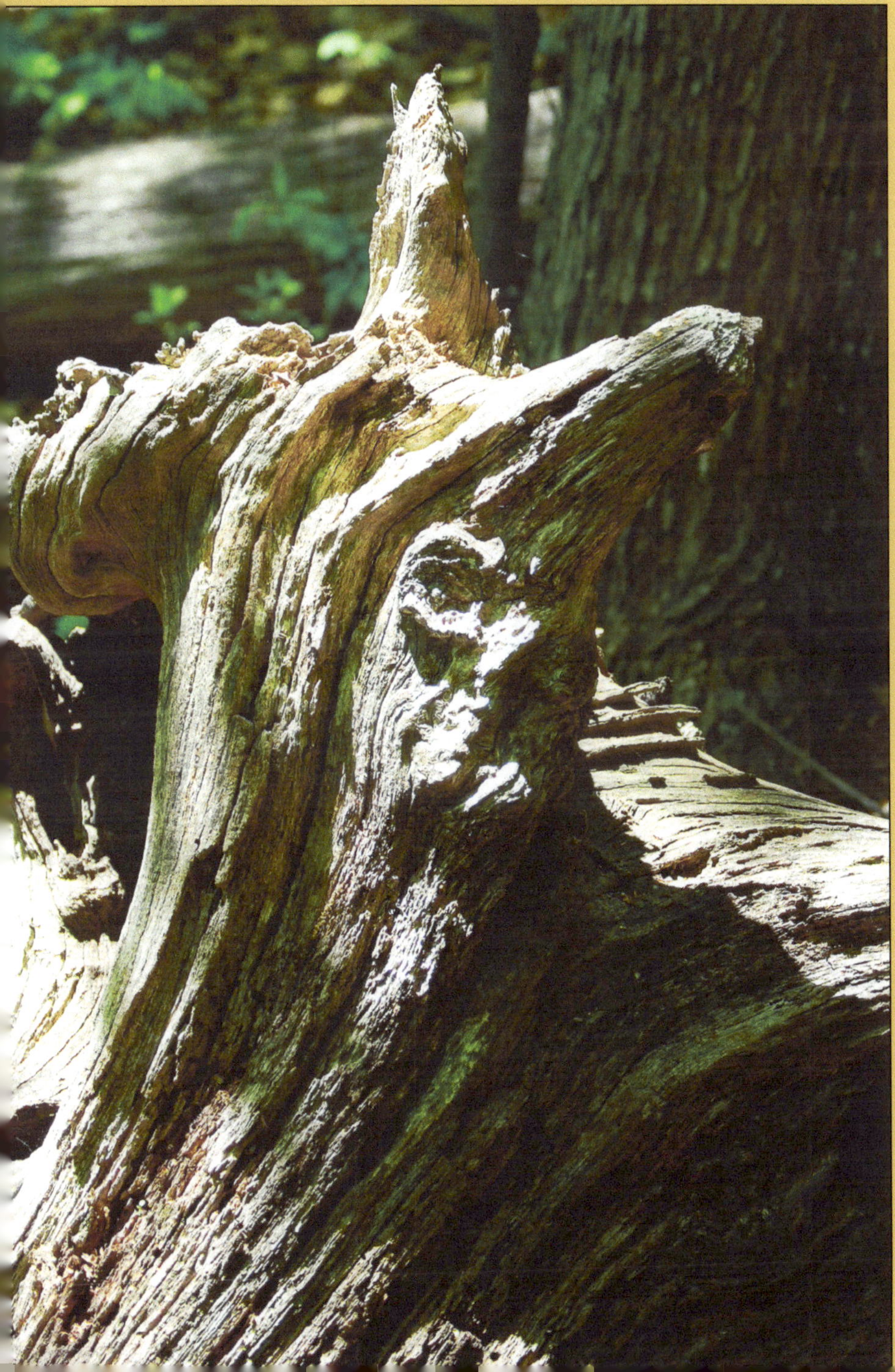

If you truly love Nature, you will find beauty everywhere.

—*Vincent Van Gogh*

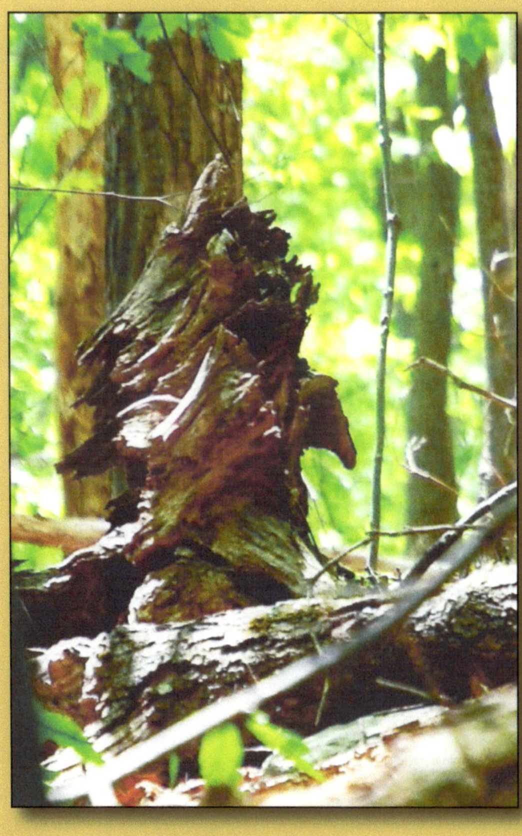

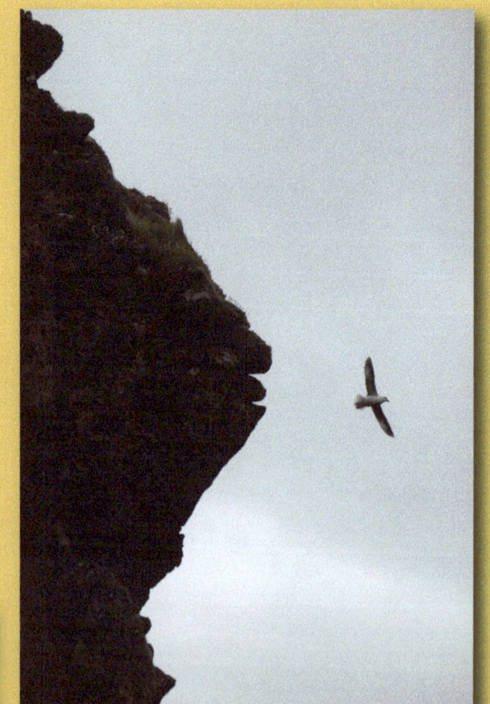
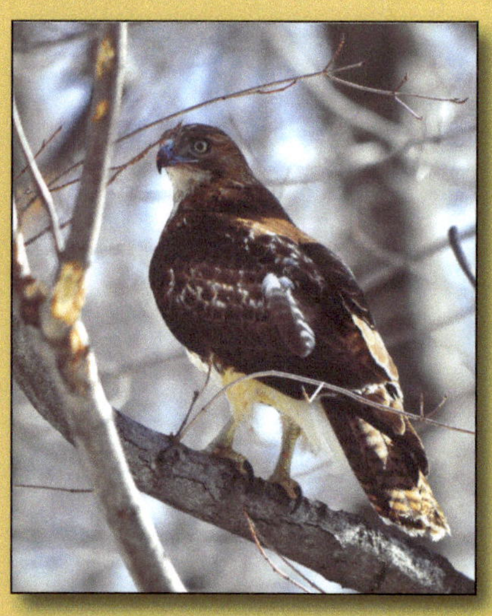
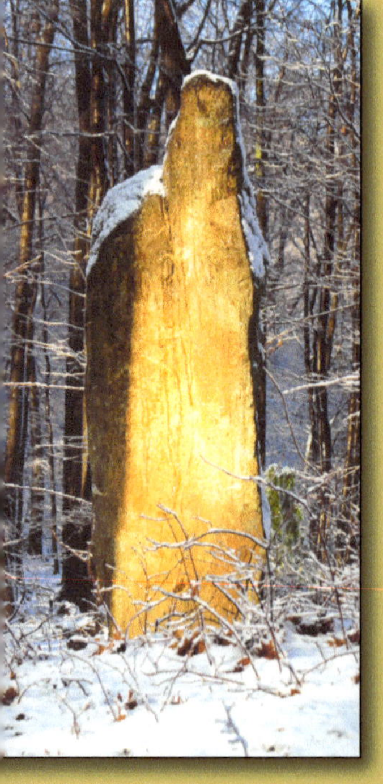
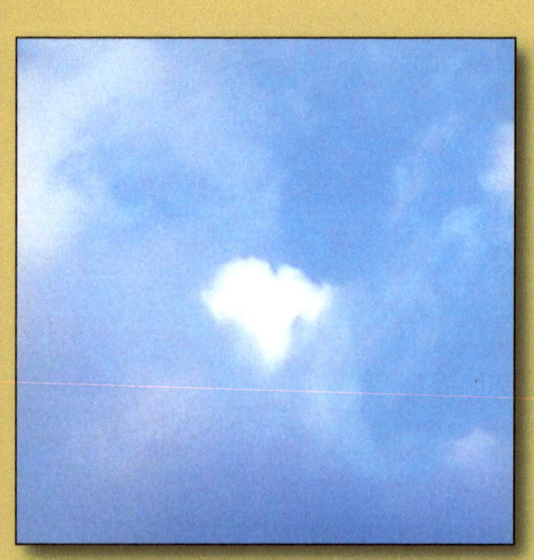
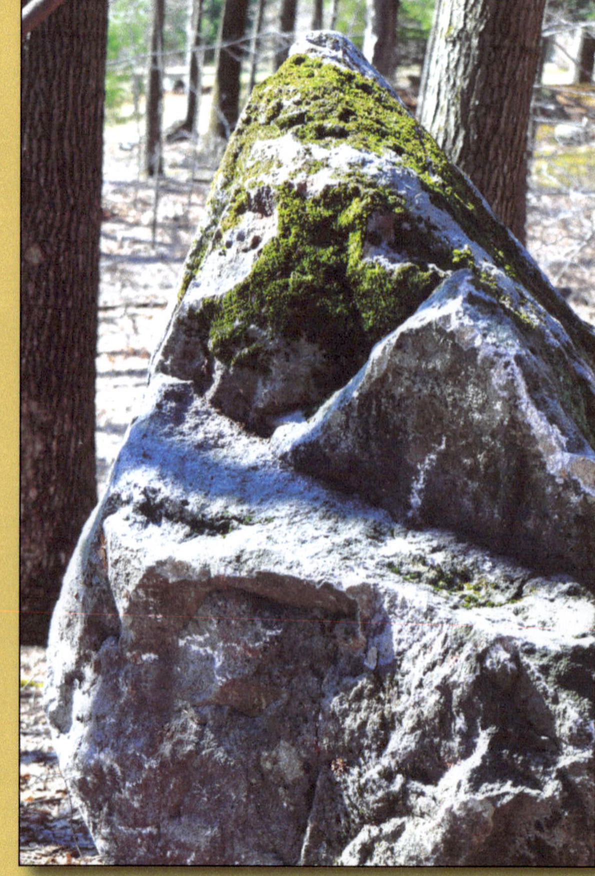
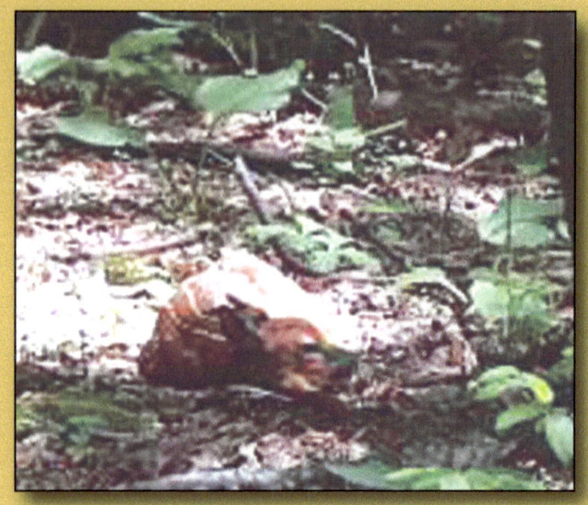
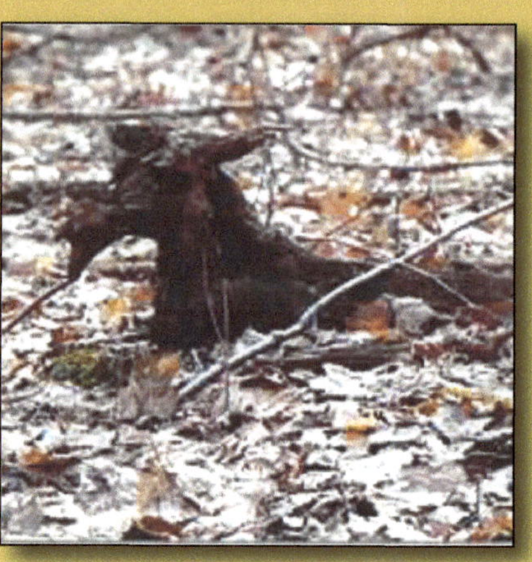

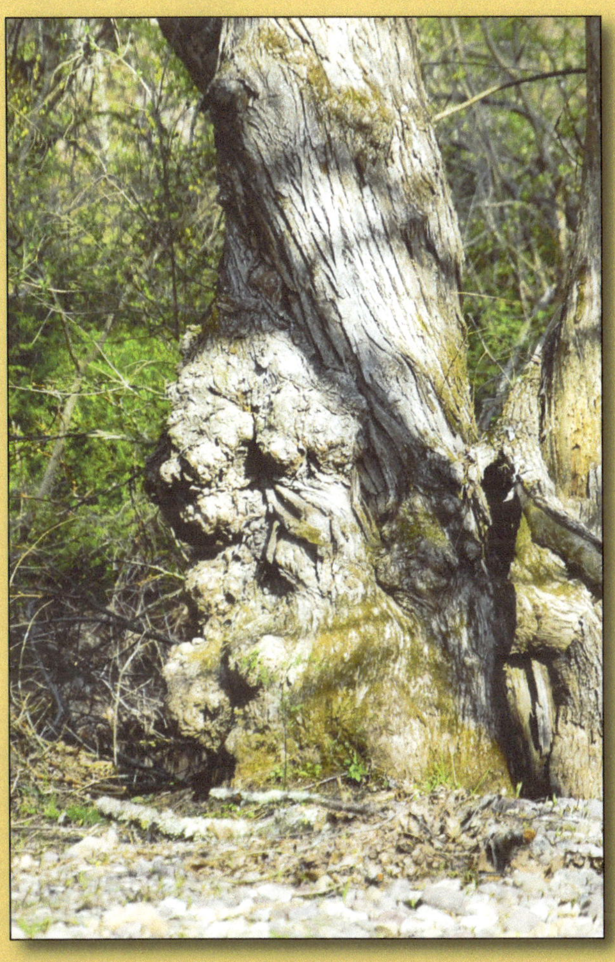

Approaching a tree we approach a sacred being who can teach us about love and about endless giving. She is one of millions of beings who provide our air, our homes, our fuel, our books. Working with the spirit of the tree can bring us renewed energy, powerful inspiration, deep communion.

—*Anon.*

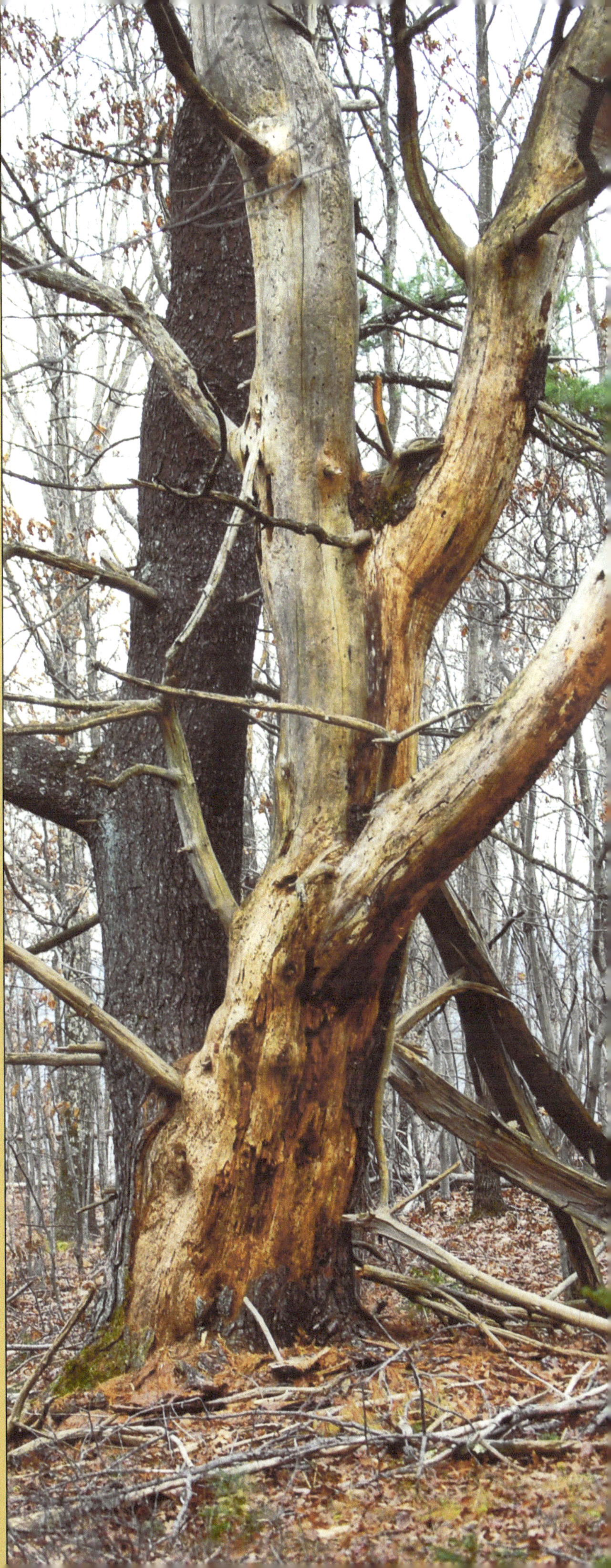

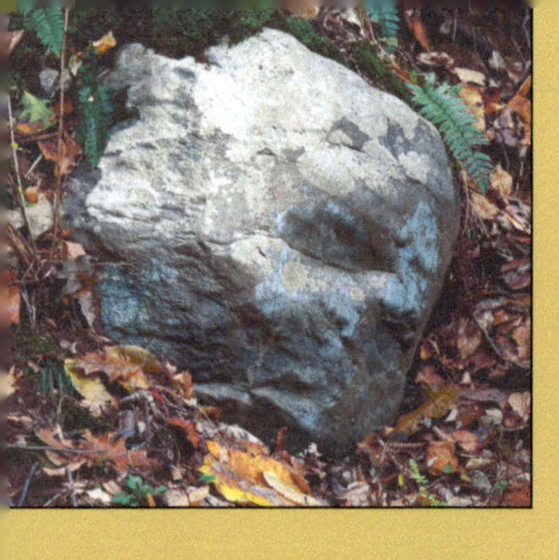
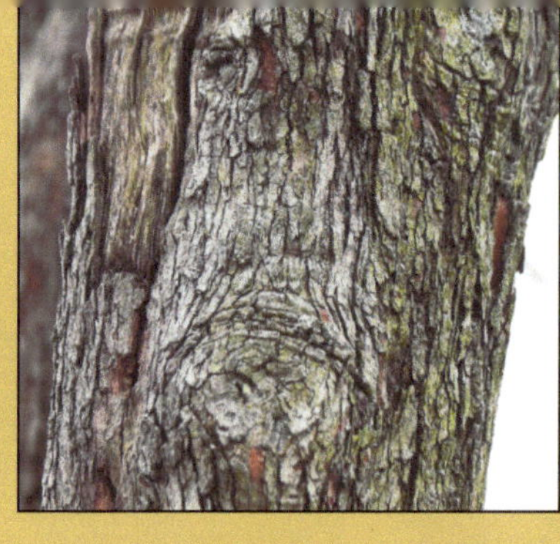
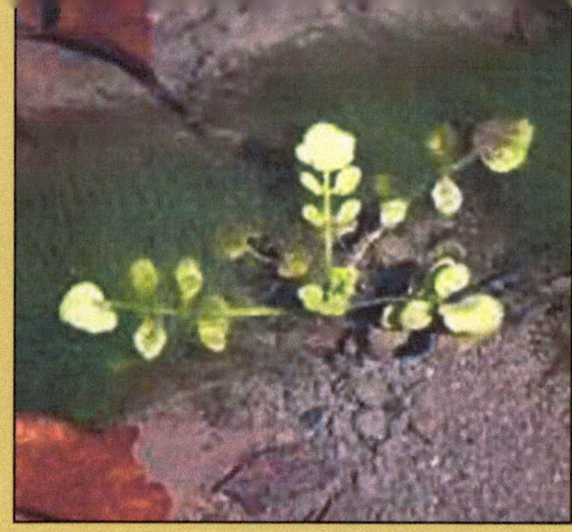
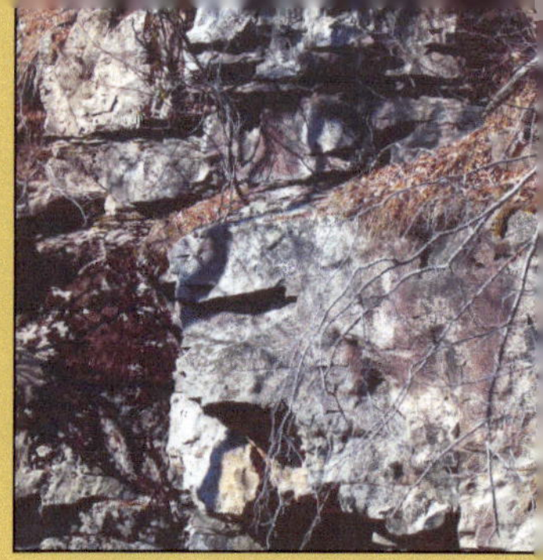
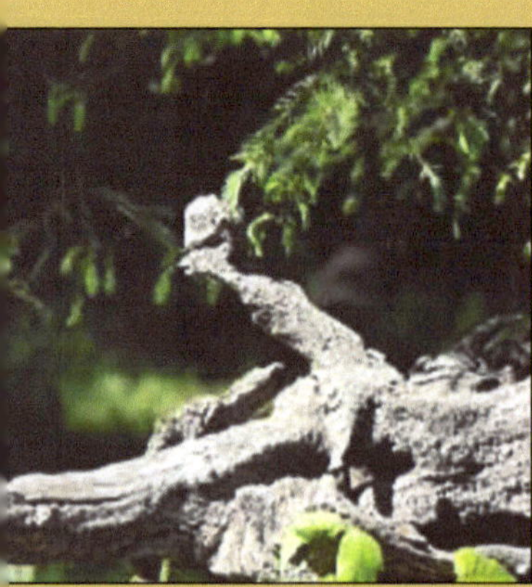

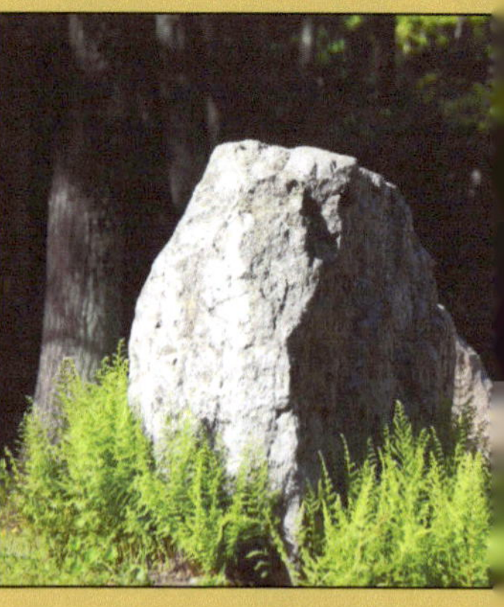
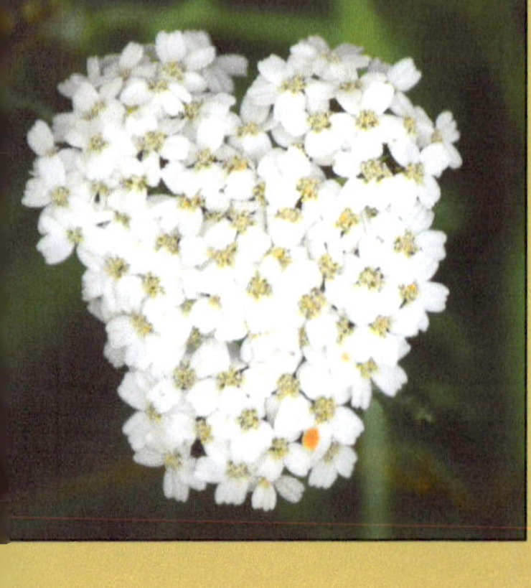
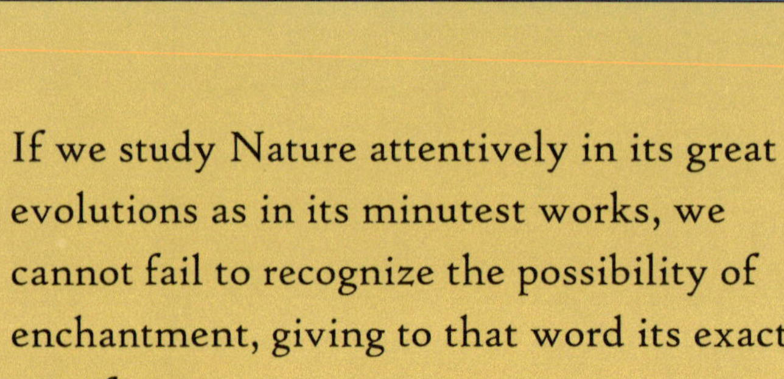

If we study Nature attentively in its great evolutions as in its minutest works, we cannot fail to recognize the possibility of enchantment, giving to that word its exact significance.

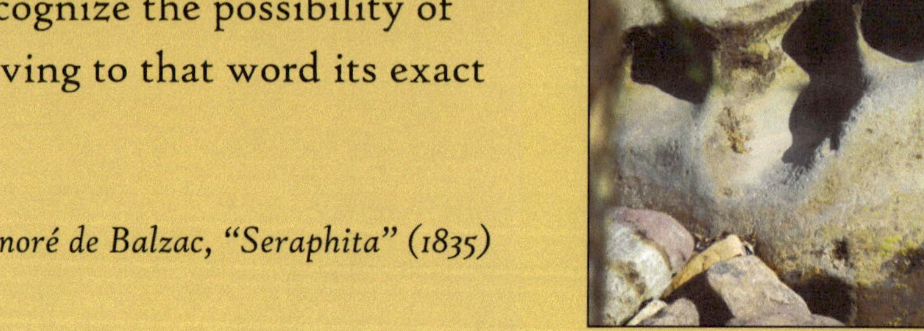
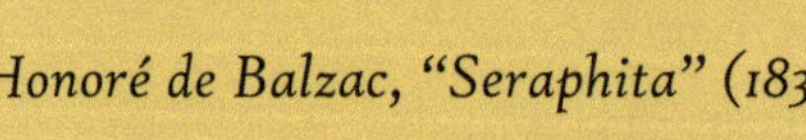

Honoré de Balzac, "Seraphita" (1835)

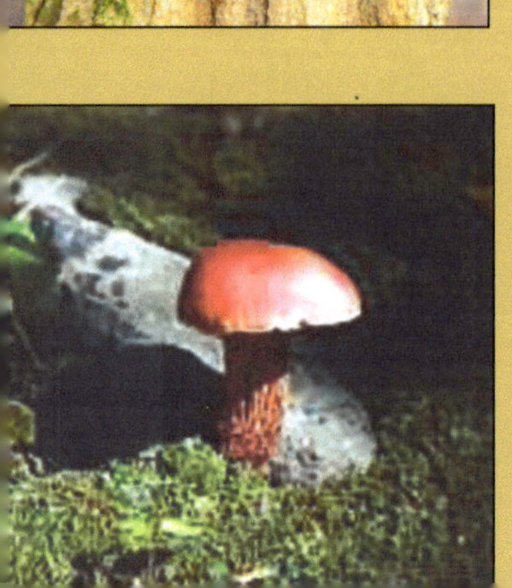
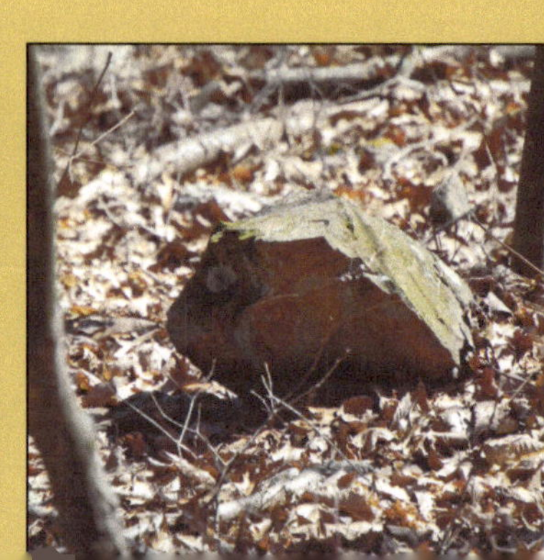
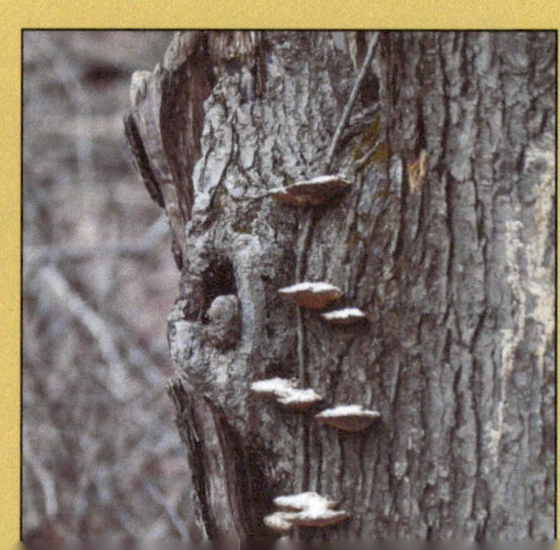
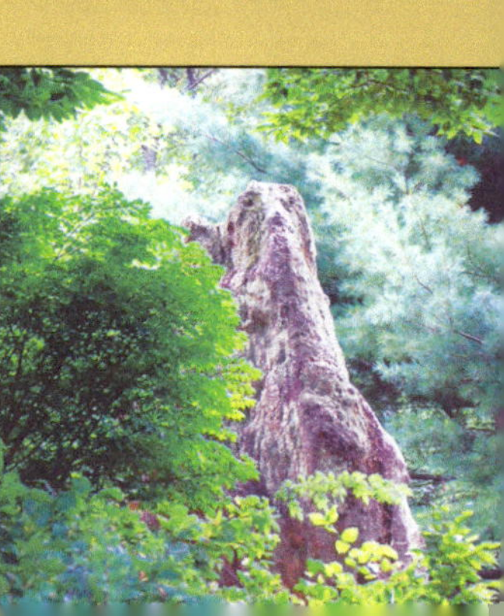

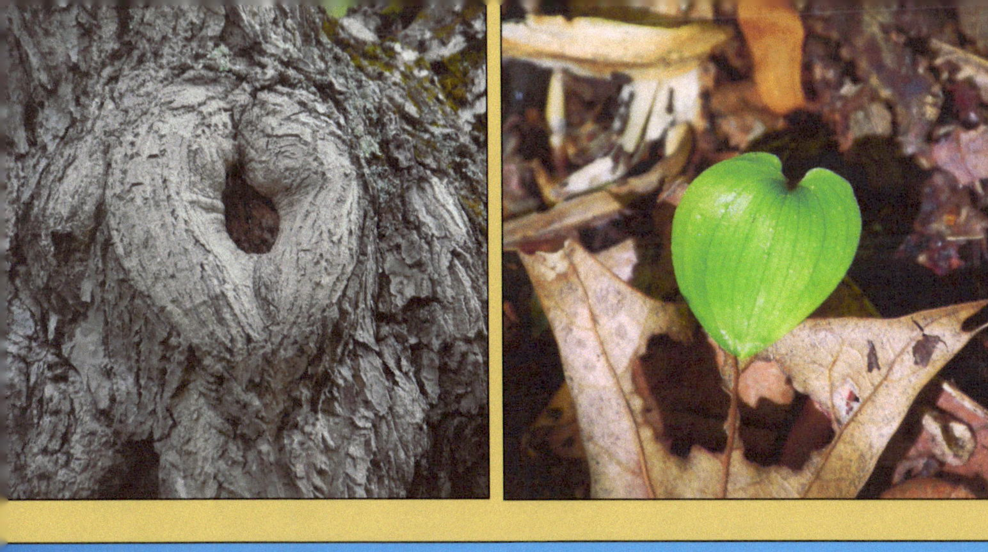

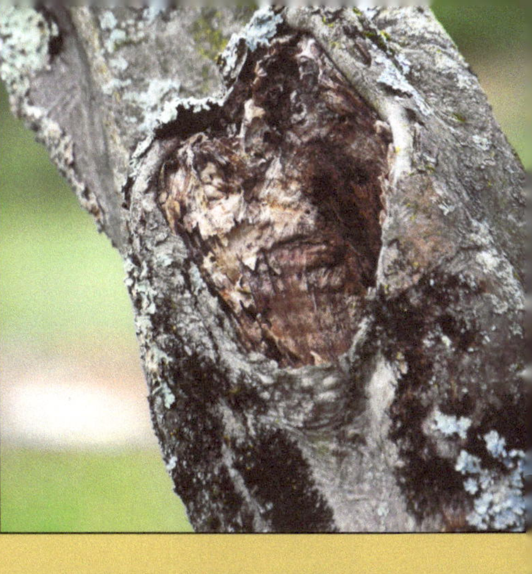

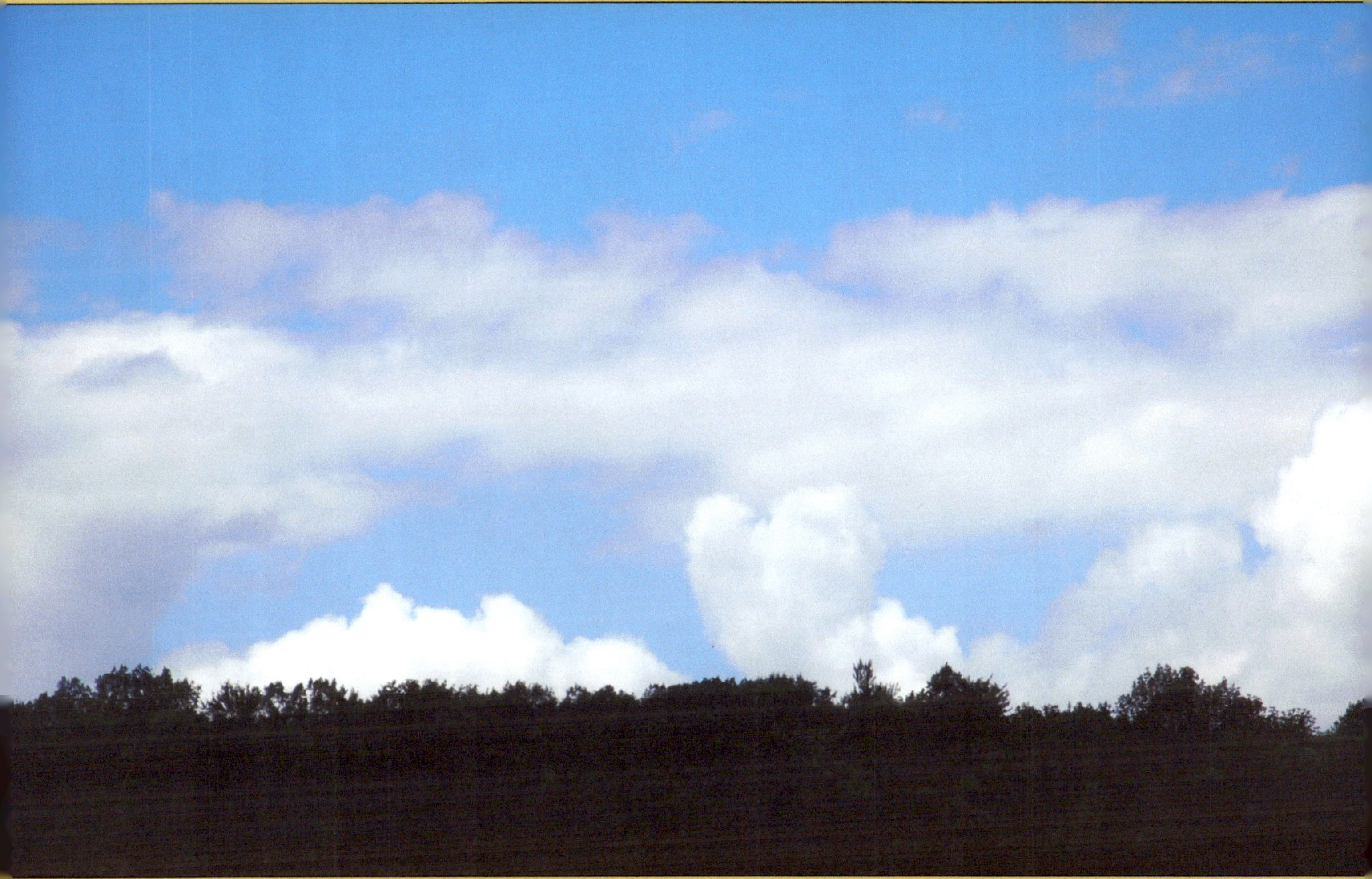

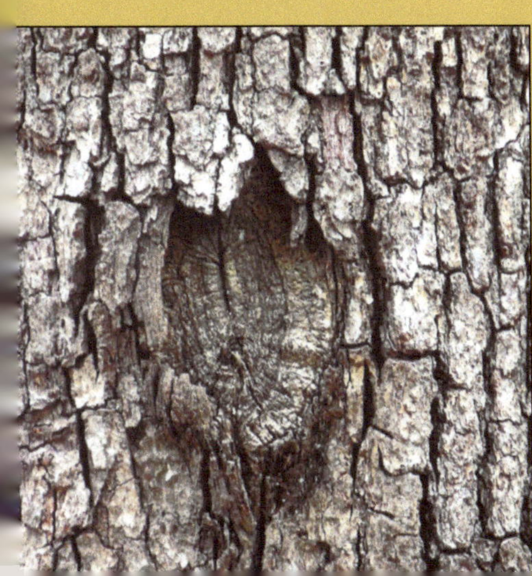

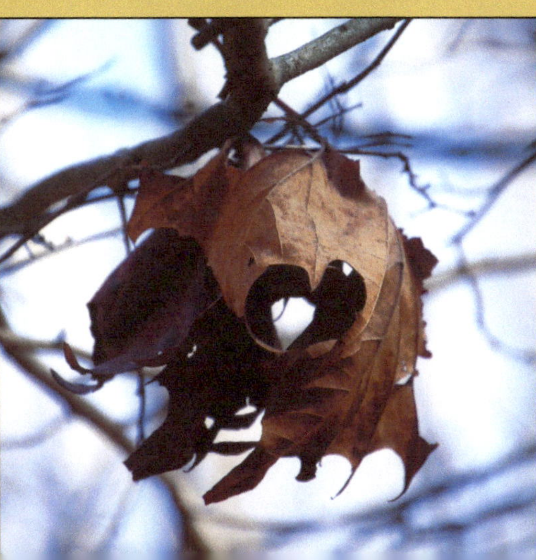

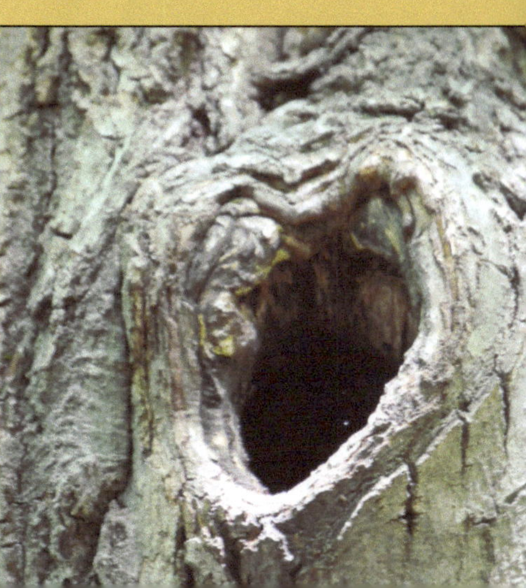

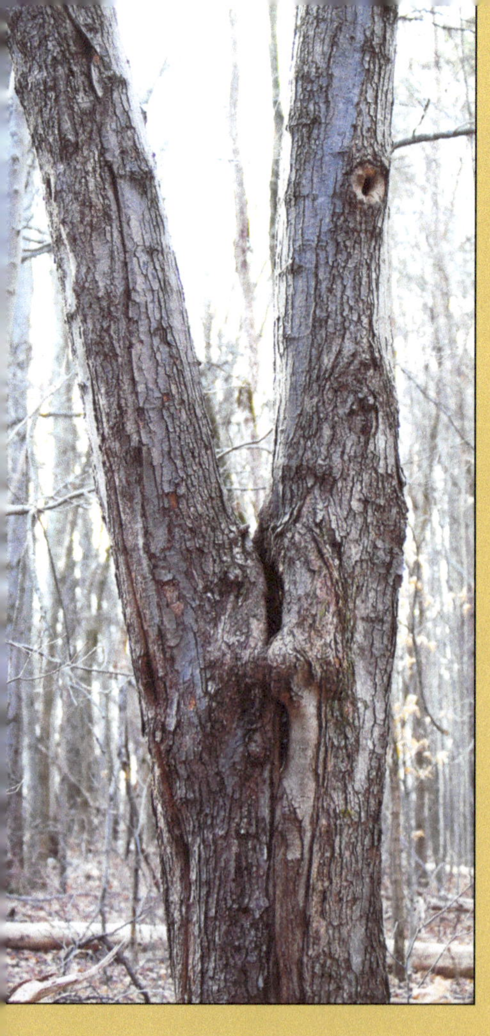

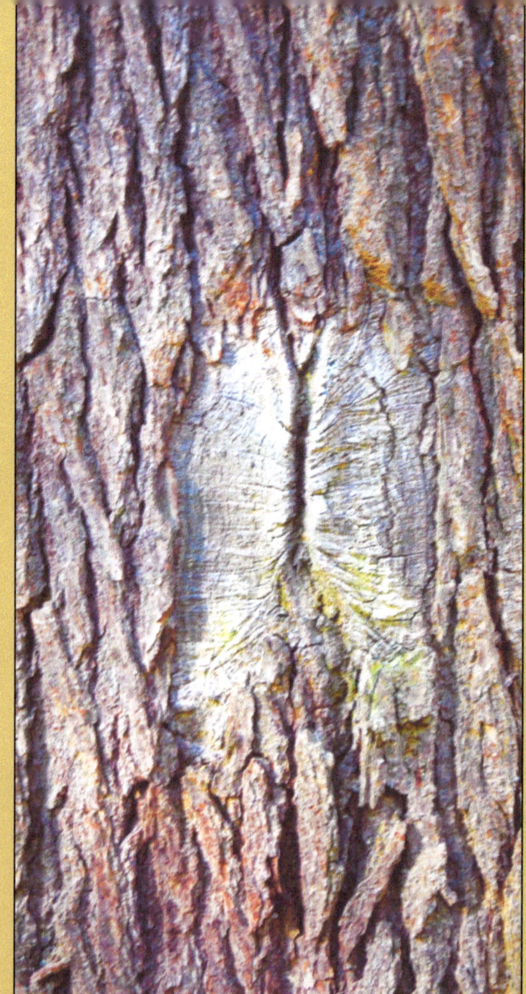

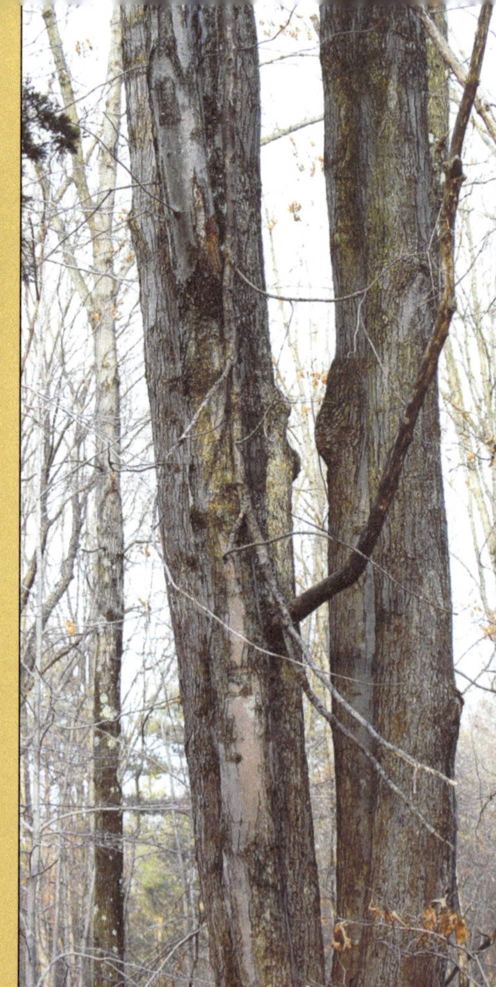

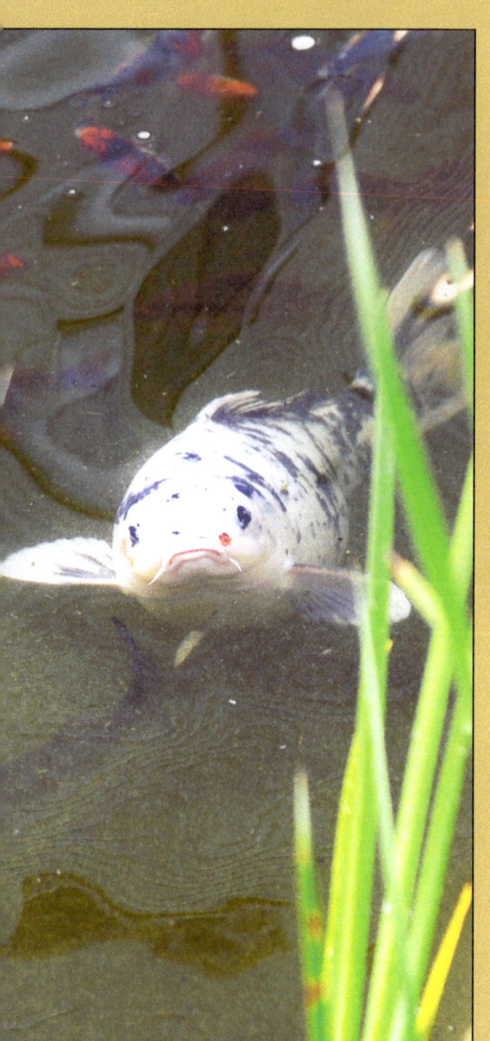

Never does nature say one thing and wisdom another.

— *Juvenal*

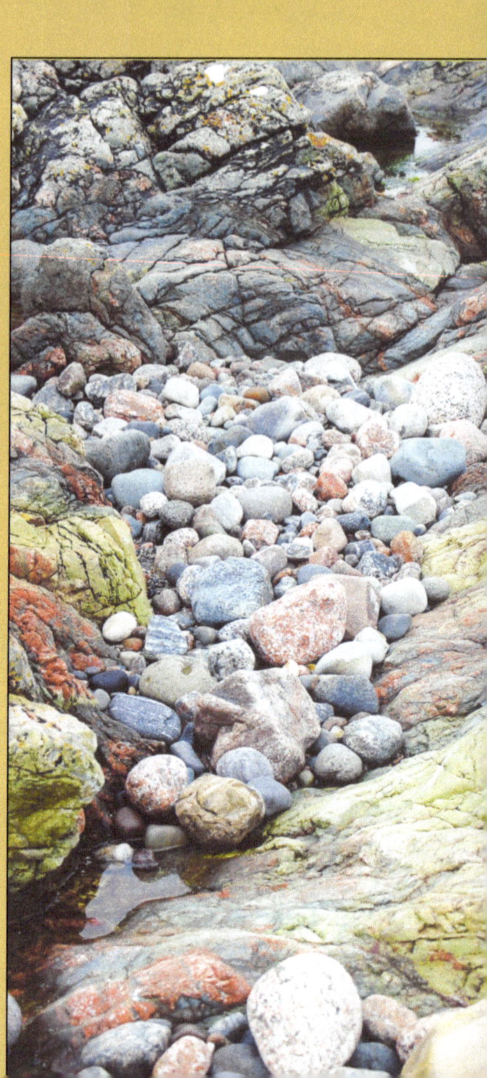

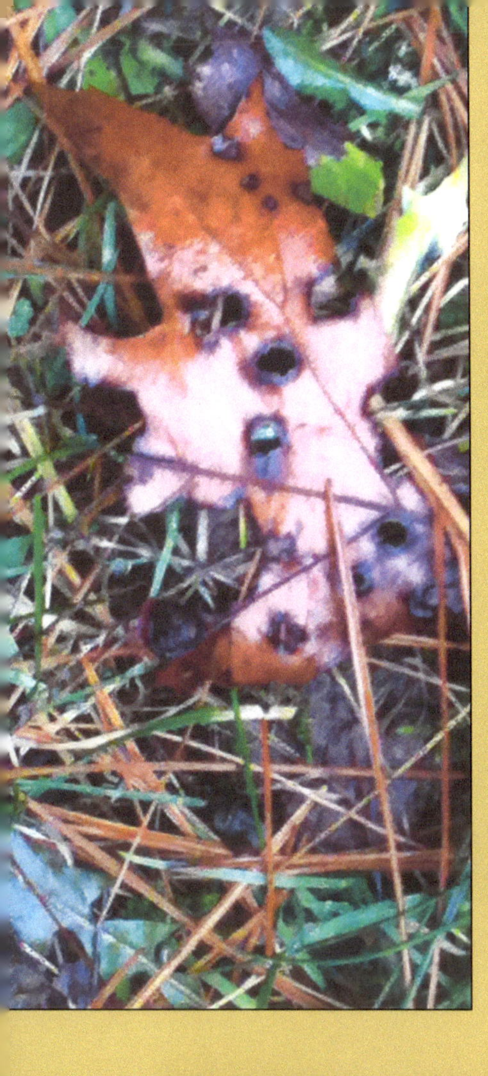
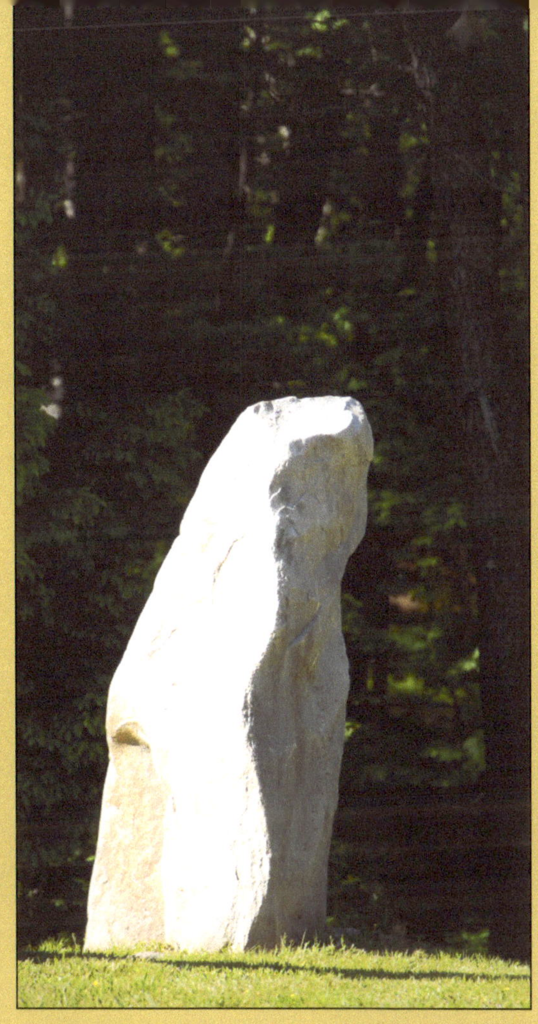
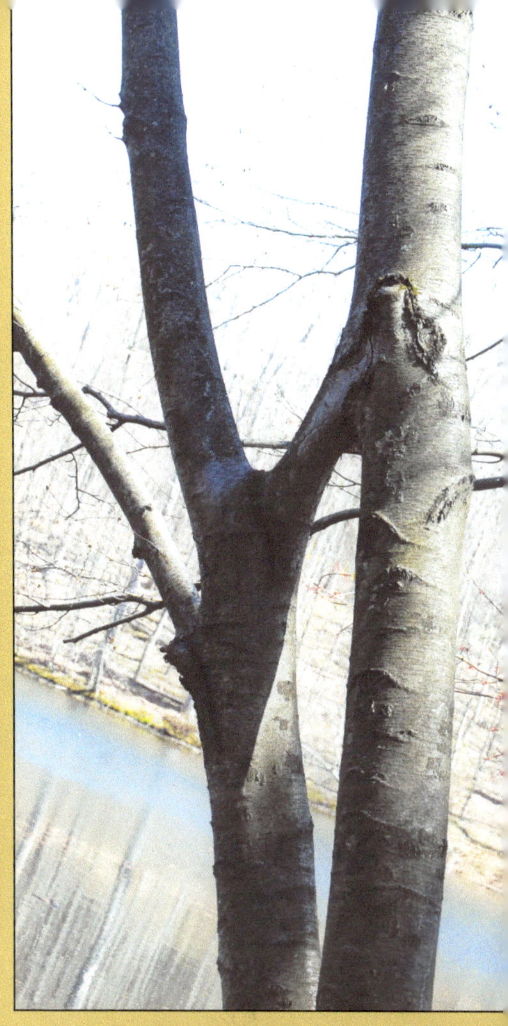
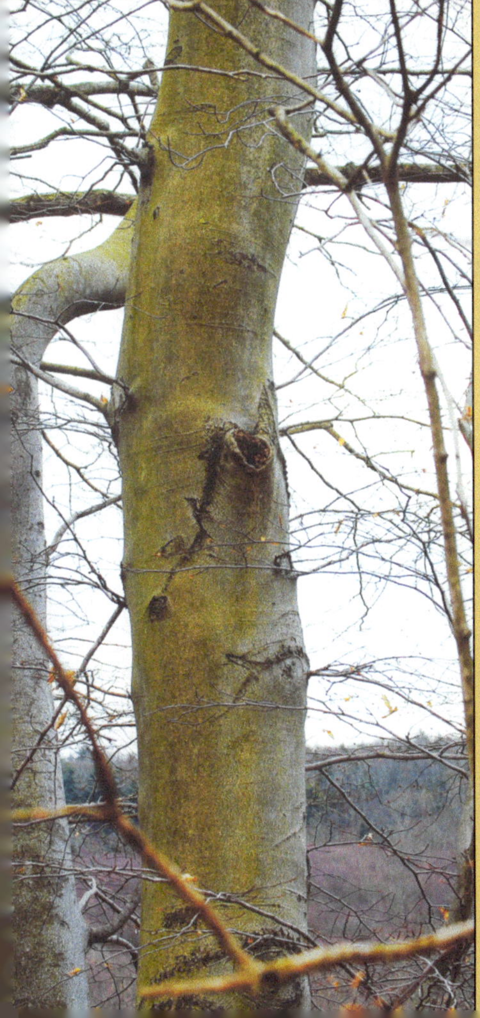
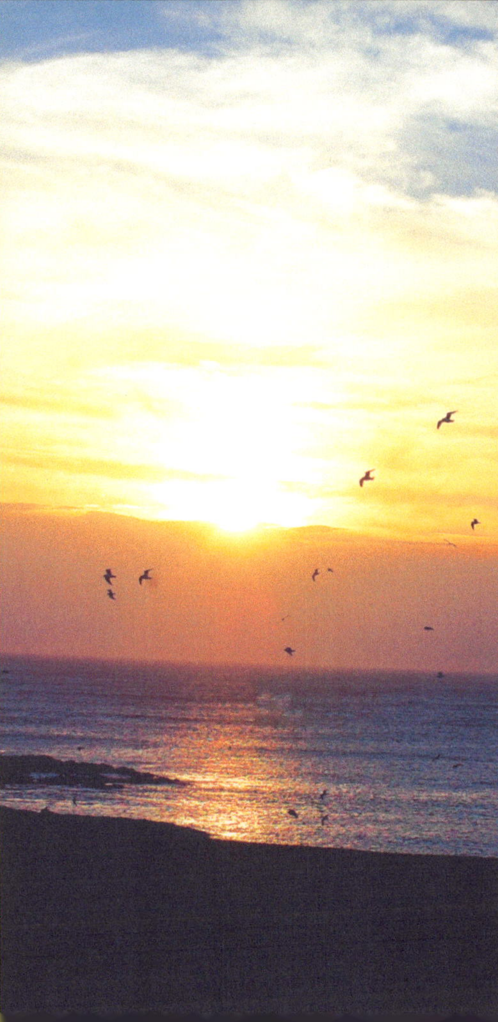
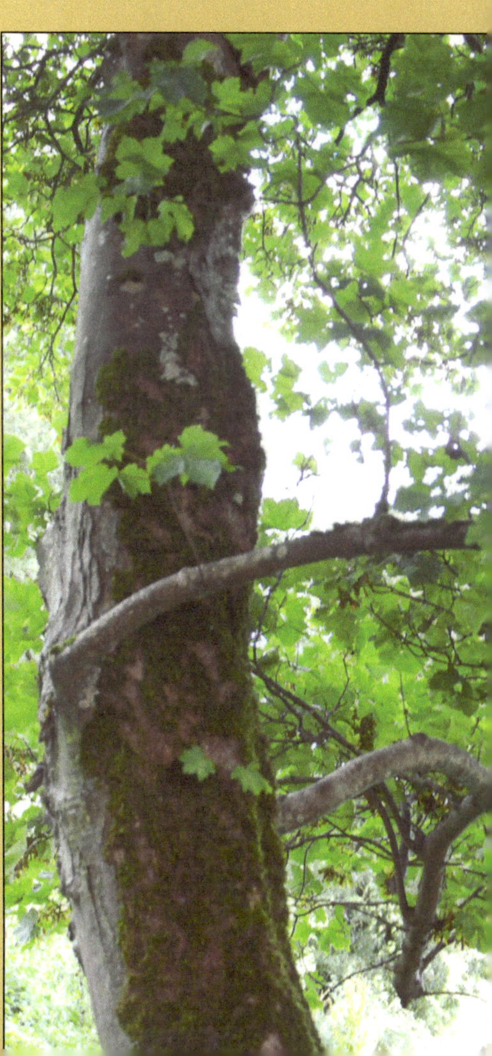

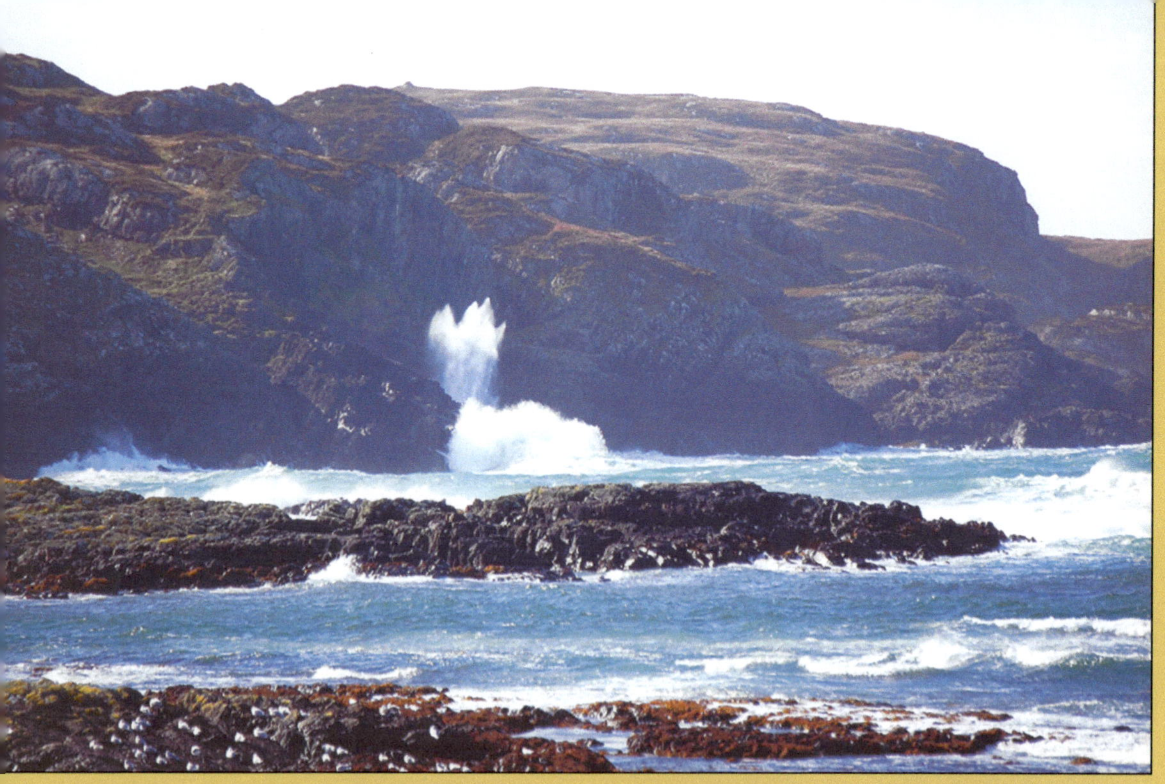

It seems to me that we all look at Nature too much, and live with her too little.

—*Oscar Wilde*

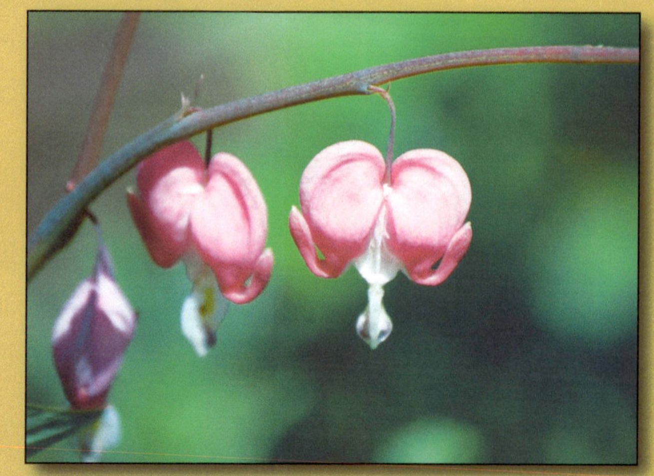

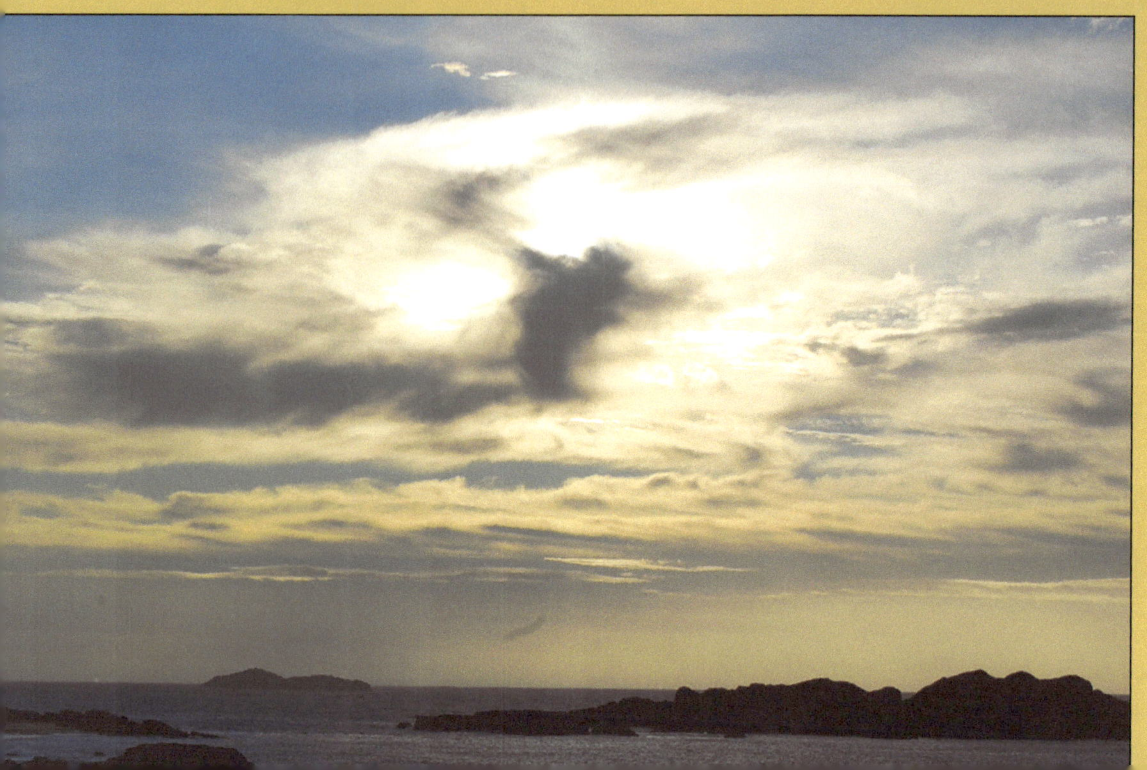

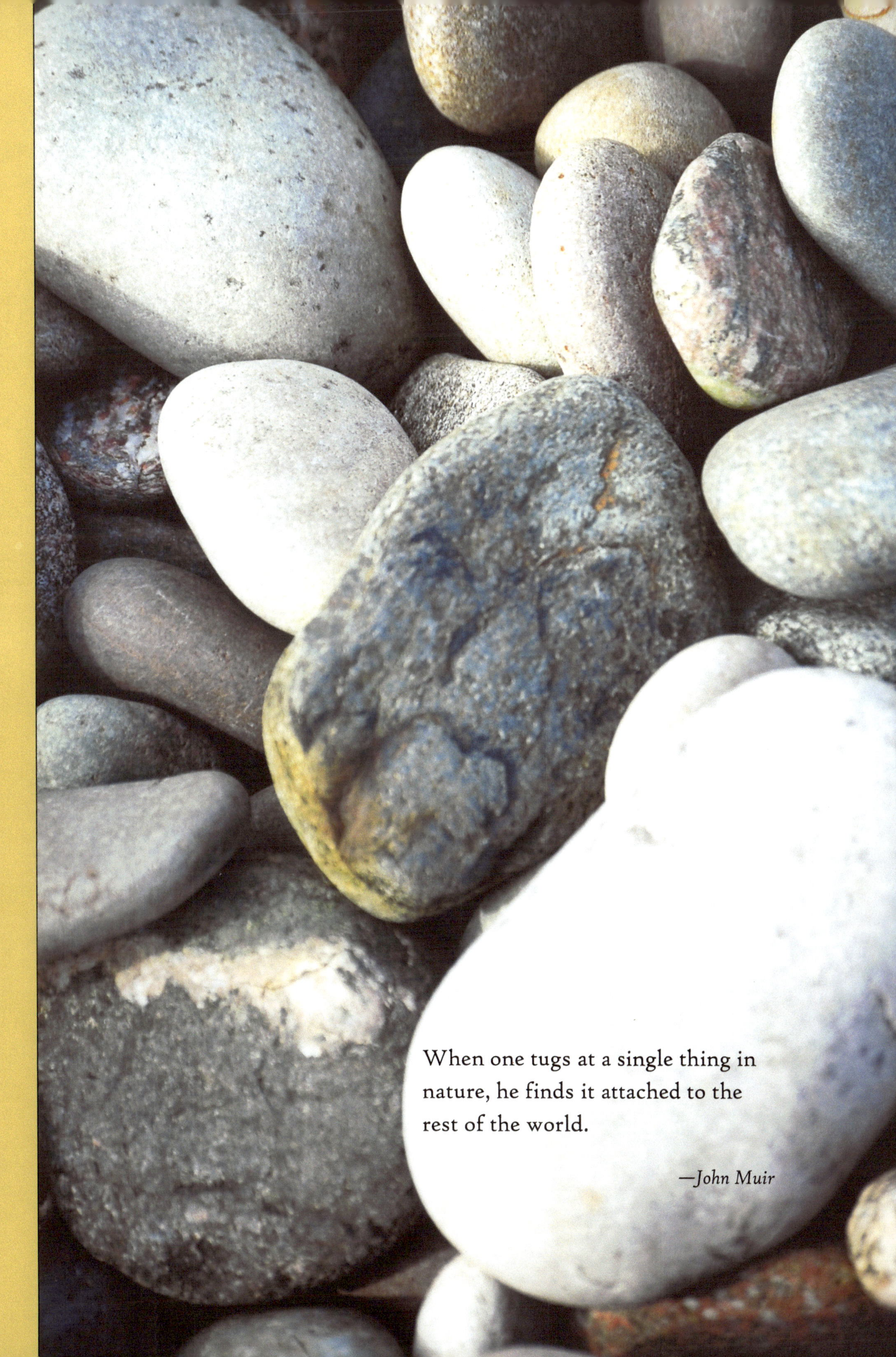

When one tugs at a single thing in nature, he finds it attached to the rest of the world.

—John Muir

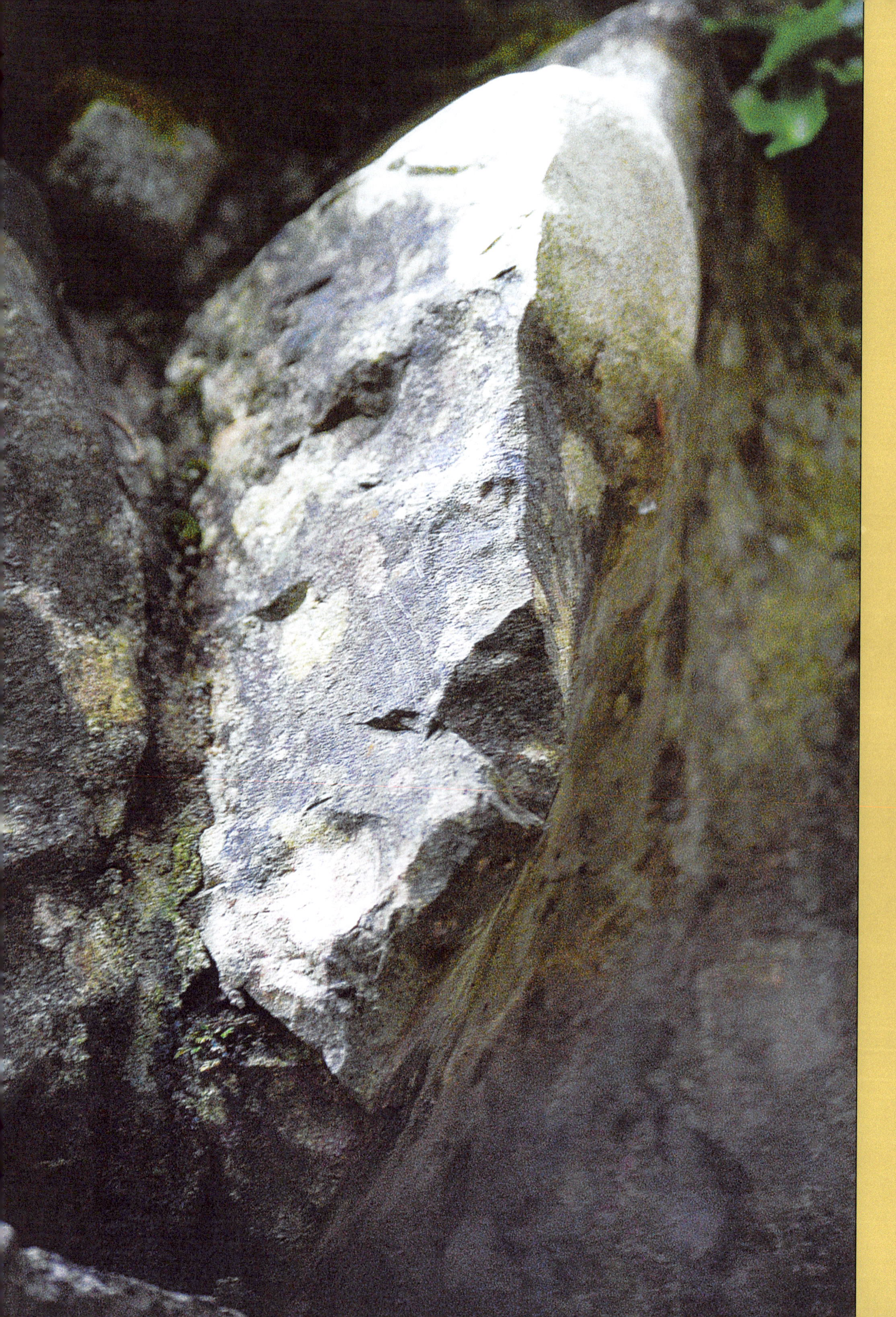

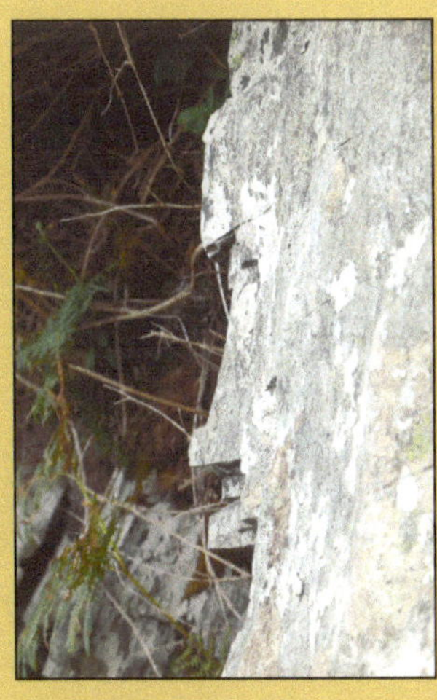

The tree which moves some to tears of joy is in the eyes of others only a green thing that stands in the way. Some see Nature all ridicule and deformity, and some scarce see Nature at all. But to the eyes of the man of imagination, Nature is Imagination itself.

—*William Blake*

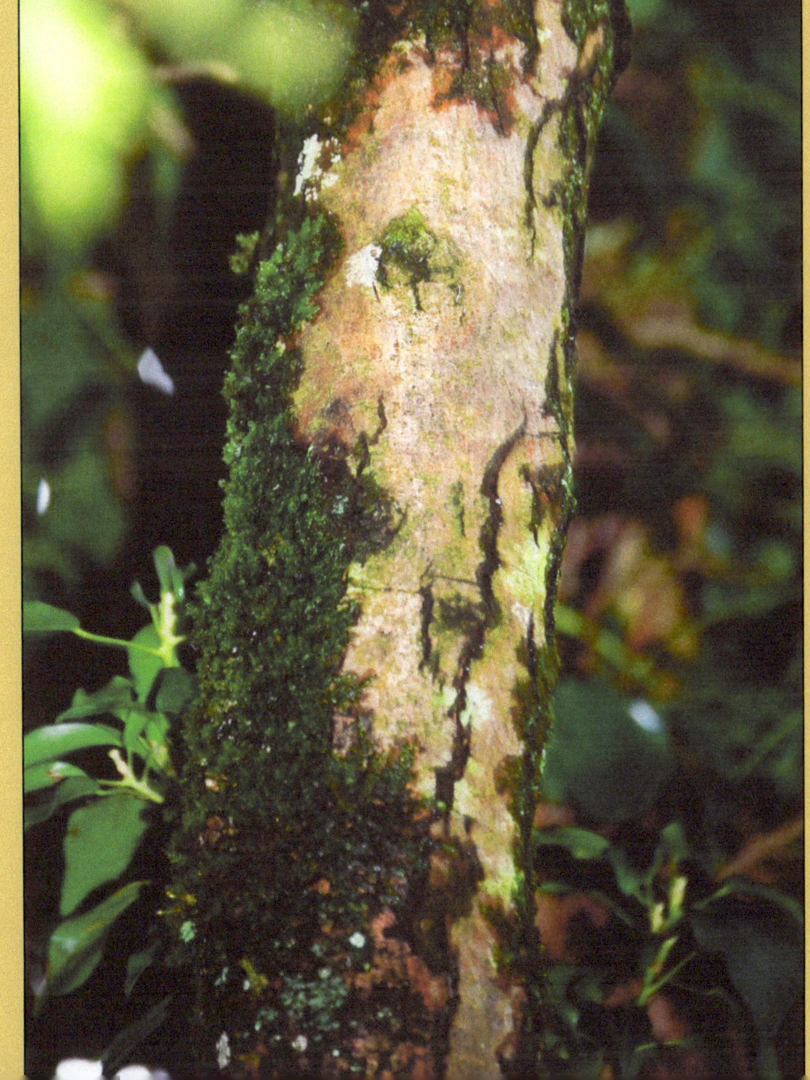

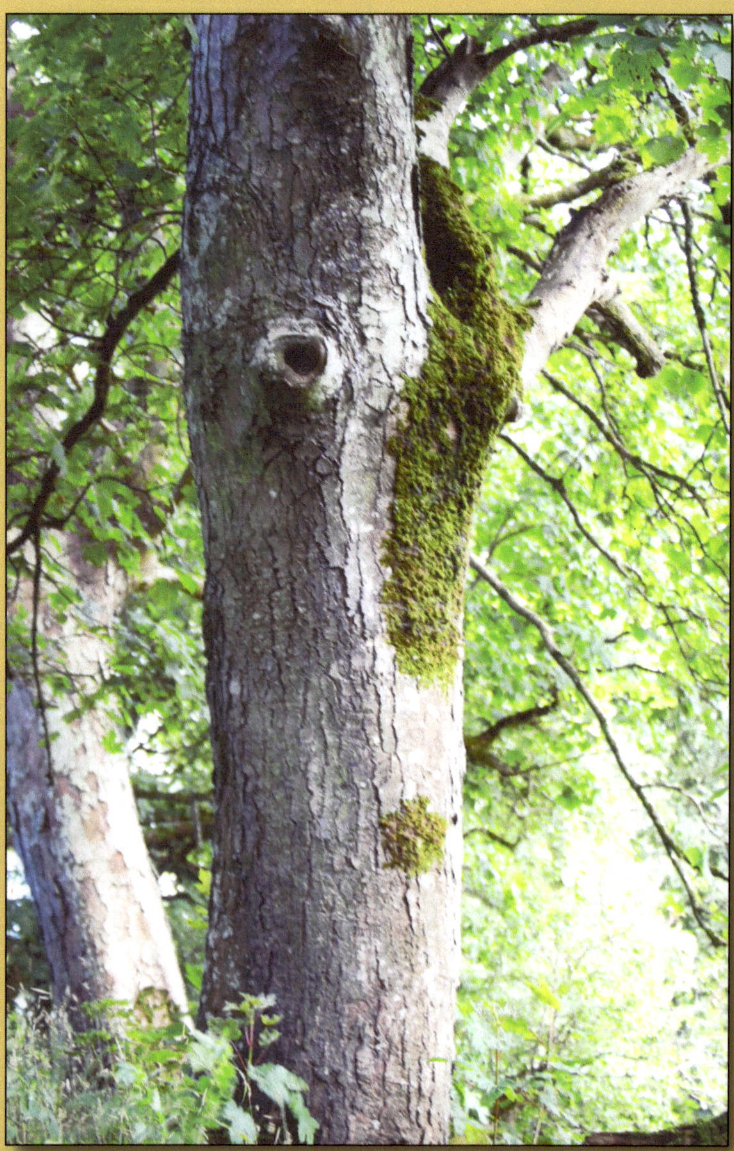

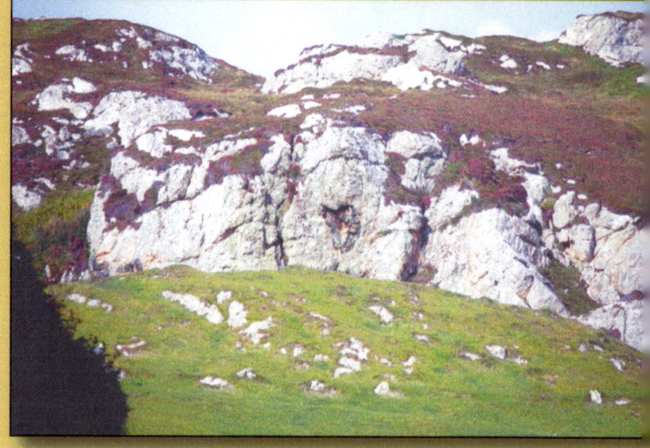

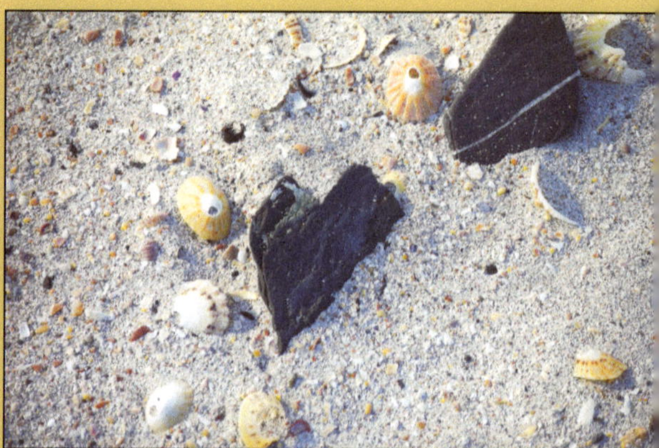

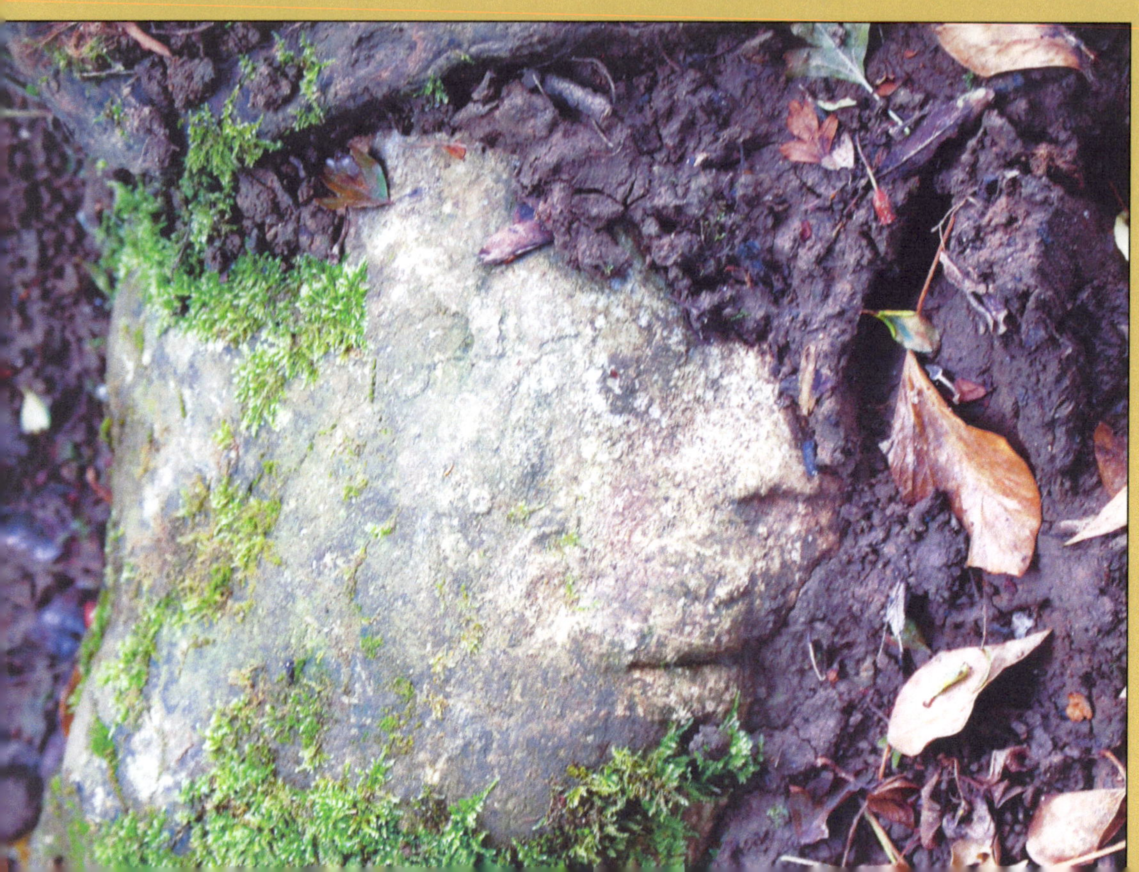

Everything has its beauty but not everyone sees it.

—*Confucius*

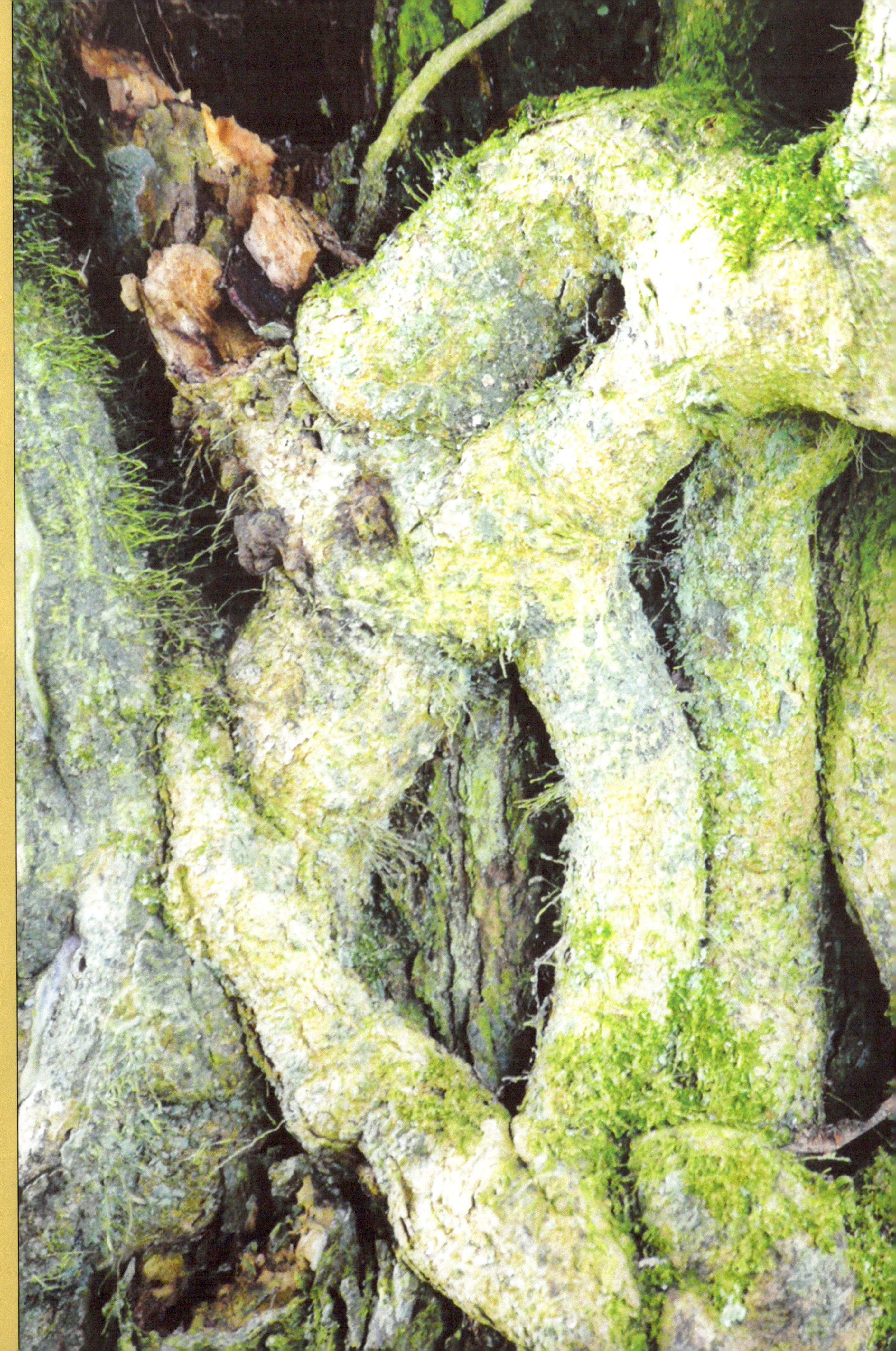

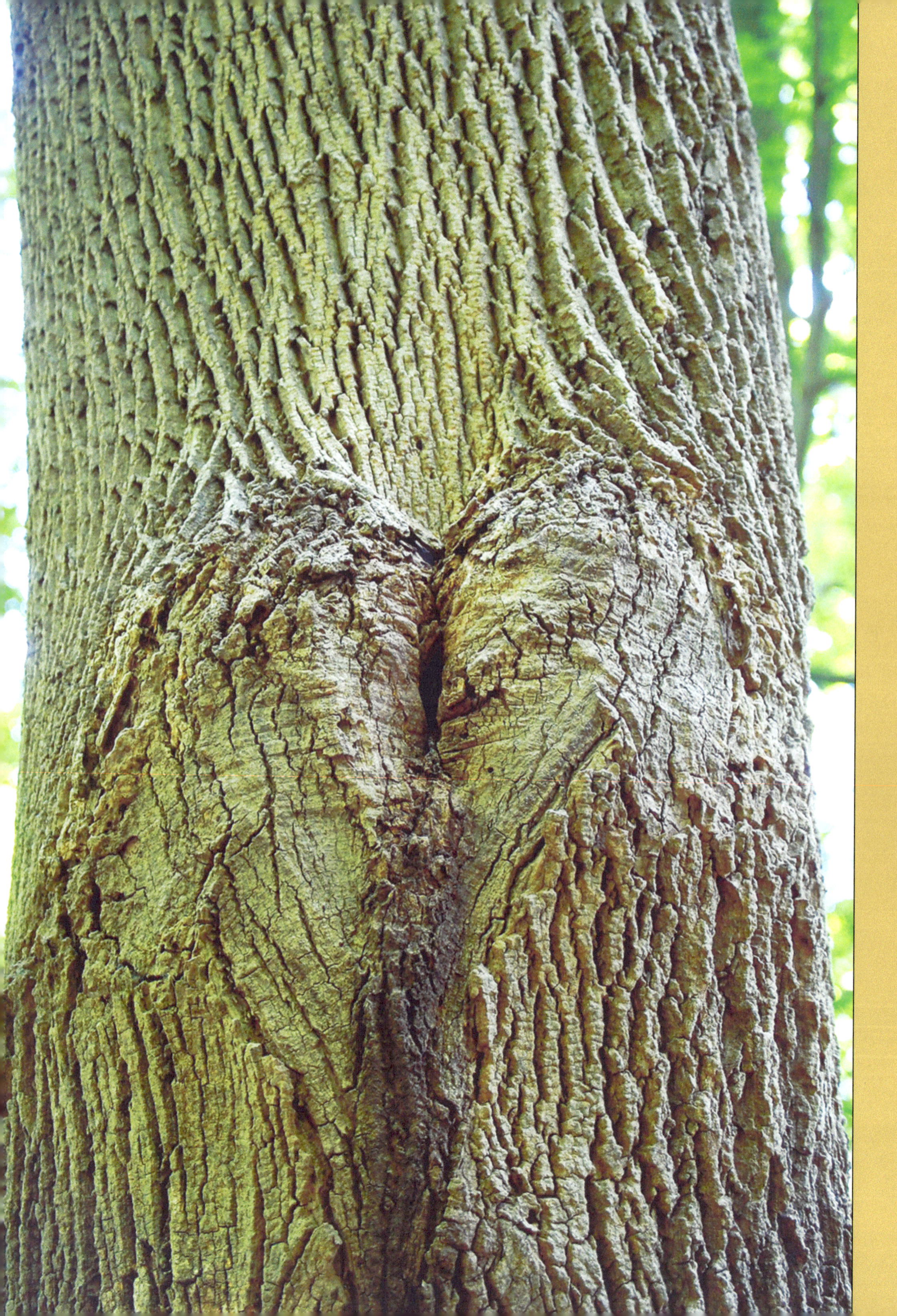

Nature does nothing uselessly.

—*Aristotle*

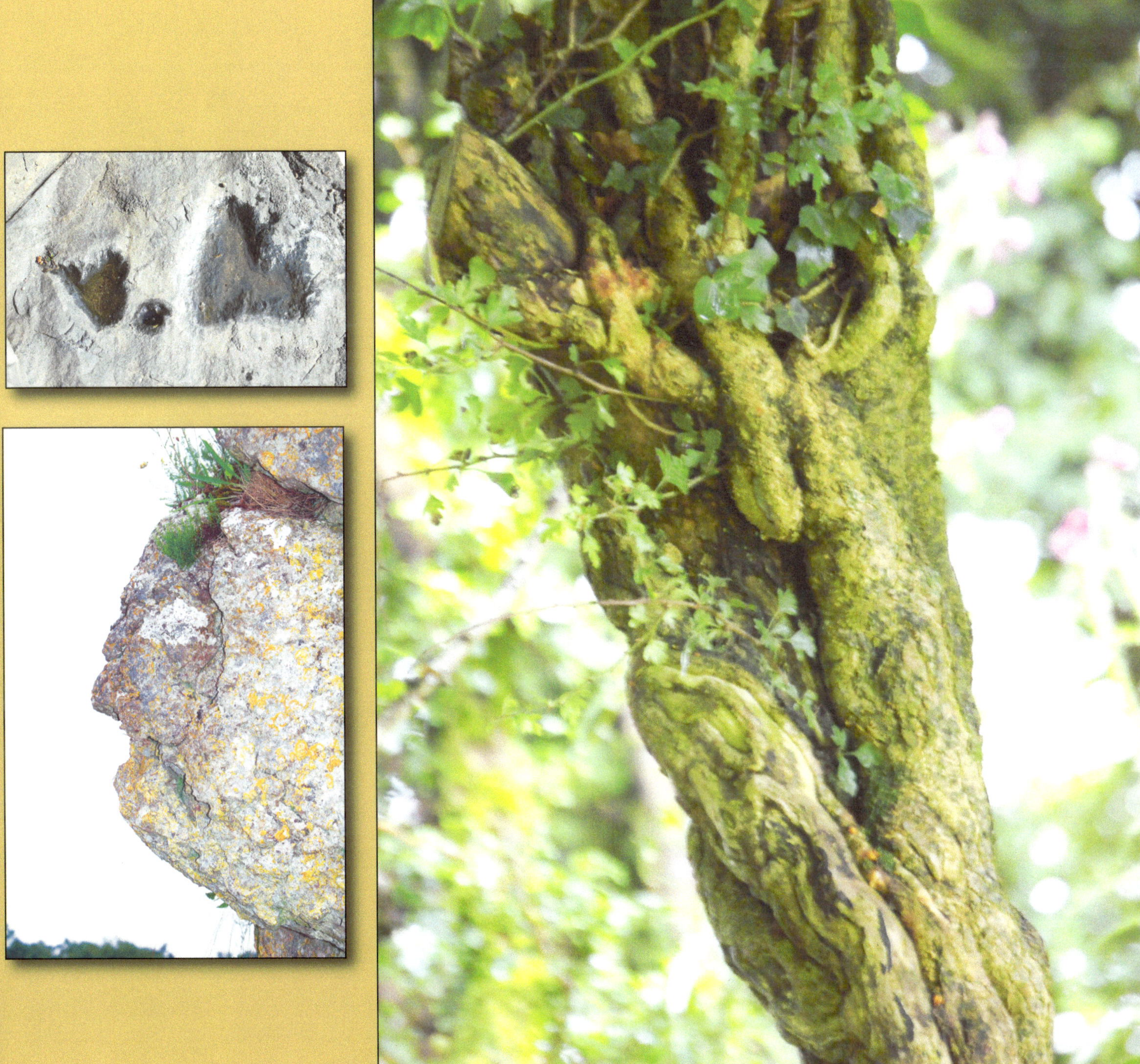

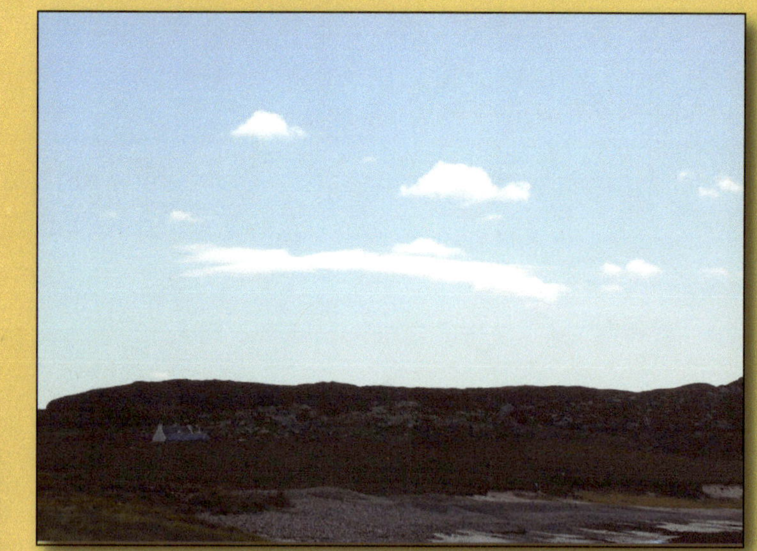

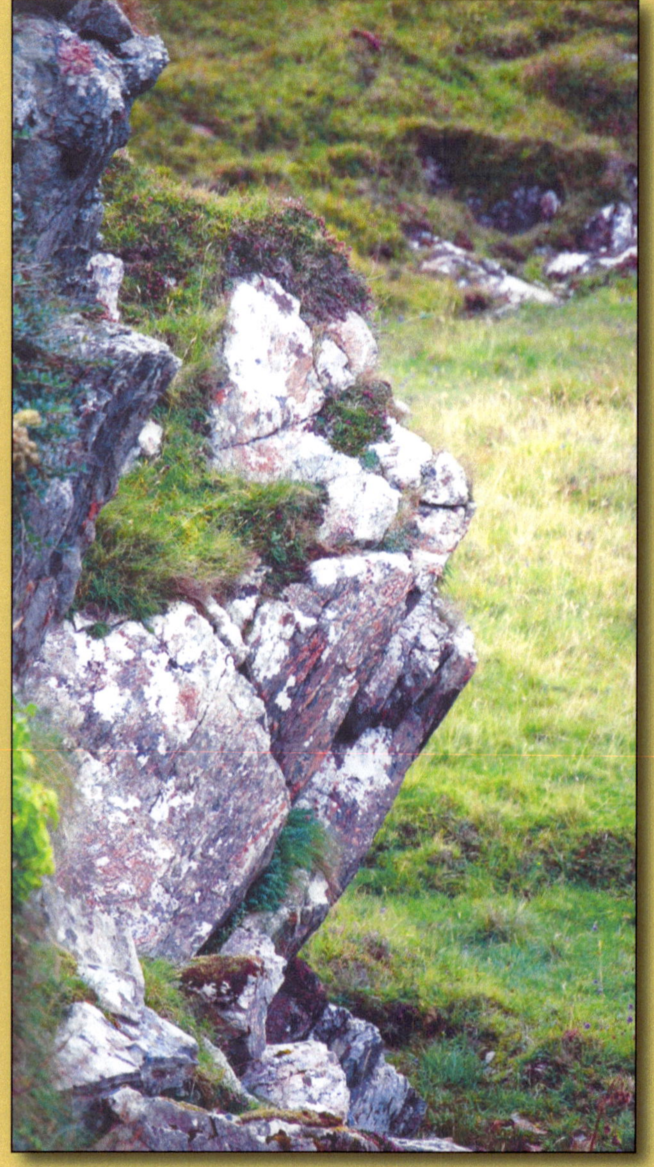

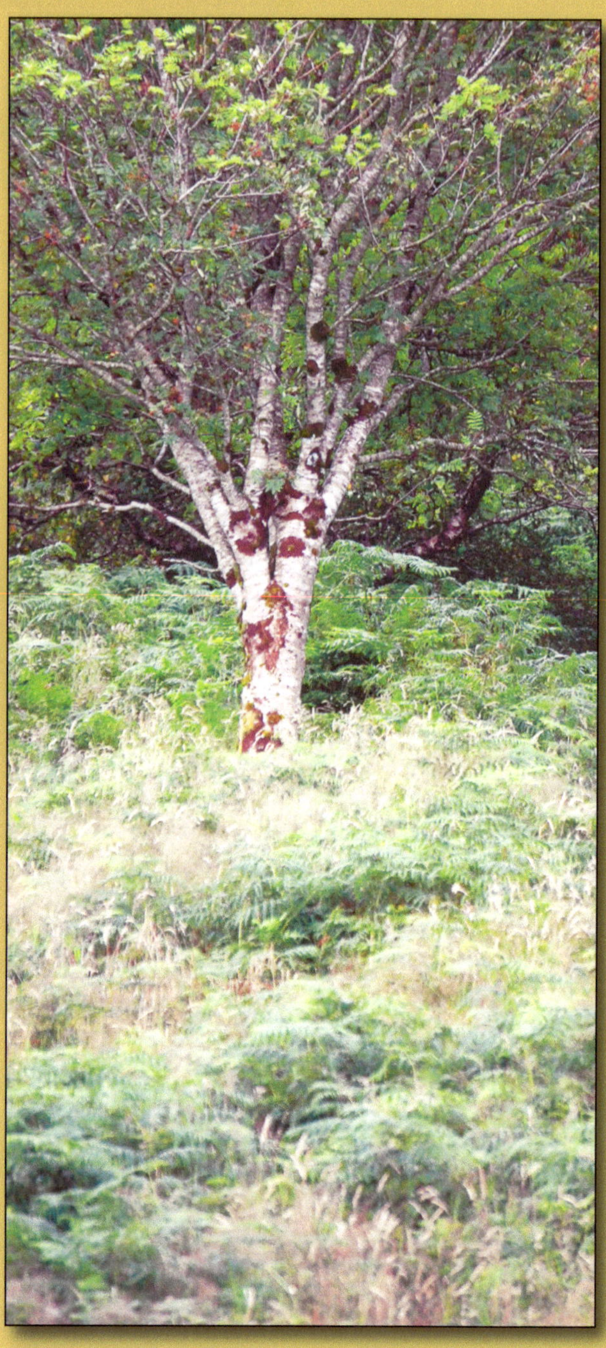

Until mankind can extend the circle of his compassion to include all living things, he will never, himself, know peace.

—*Albert Schweitzer*

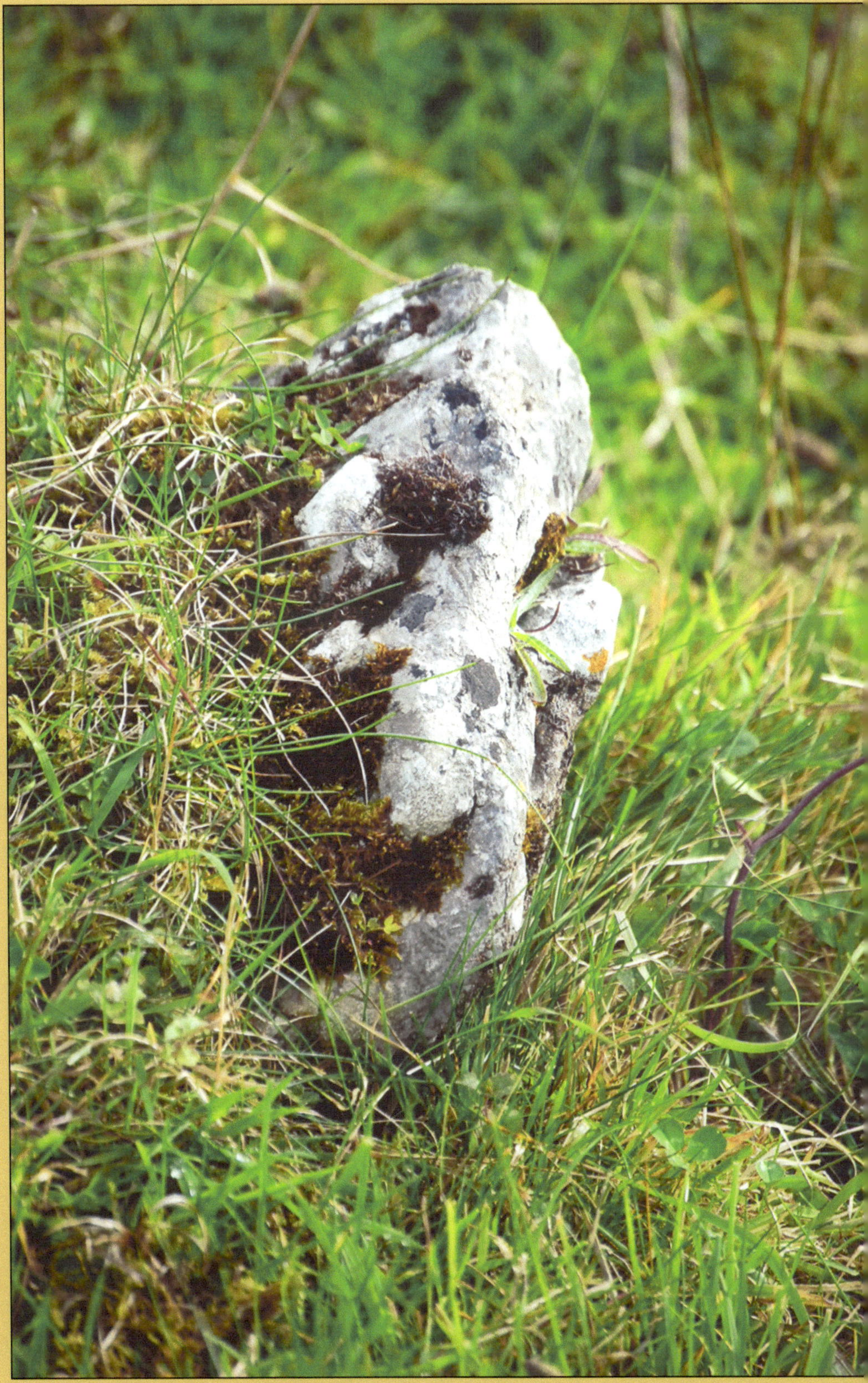

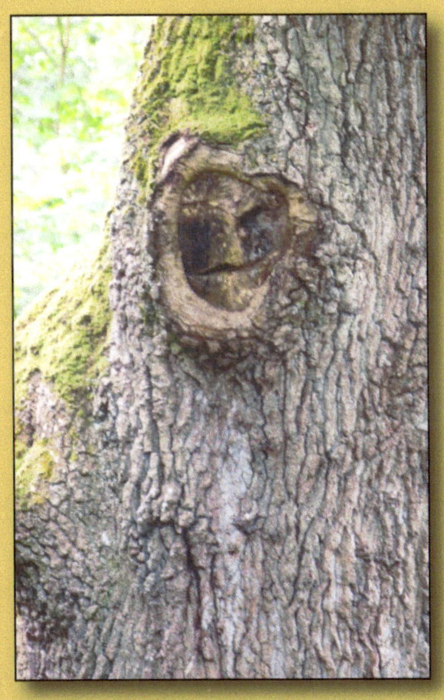

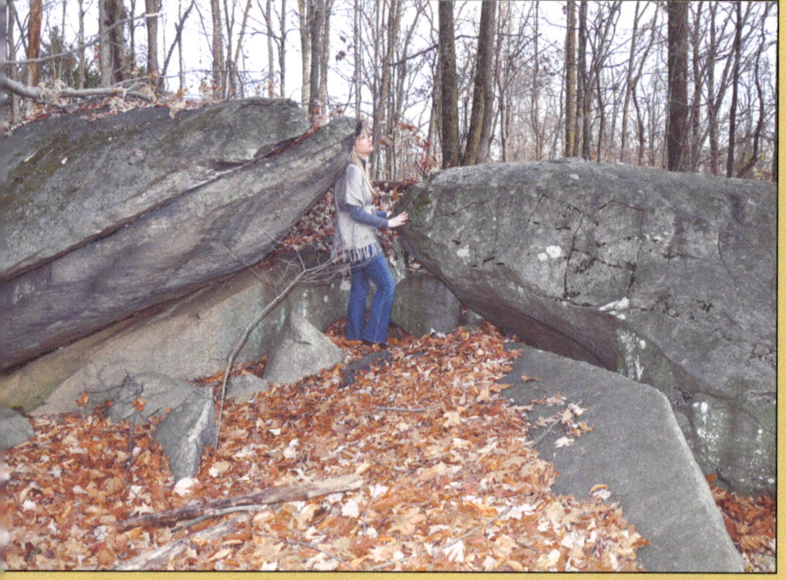

I want to offer a special acknowledgment to my family, friends, mentors, and guides who accompanied me both physically and spiritually along the way while creating this book.

This book literally flowed into being as if it had a mission or a message of its own. Perhaps it is simply to serve as a reminder that we are never alone, that we are all indeed one with all life and with the Divine Source that connects us.

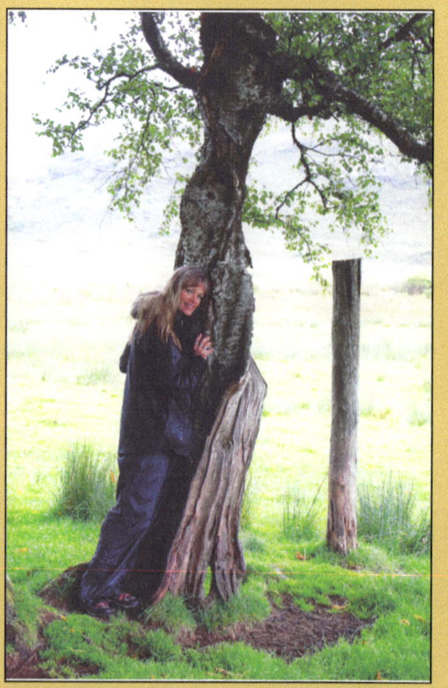

As you close this book and venture out of the forest and back into your everyday world, remember what you discovered and felt here today. Reflect on the precious life-lessons nature offers us daily; the value of silence and stillness; continual growth, both visible and from within; balance and respect of individuality within community; the cycle of death and rebirth; and so much more. I hope you go forward looking for signs and faces everywhere—in the park, in the woods, in the water, in the sky, even on city streets. The sacred is everywhere, in every living being and in you. You will never stand alone if you remember to "walk awake."

—QofF*

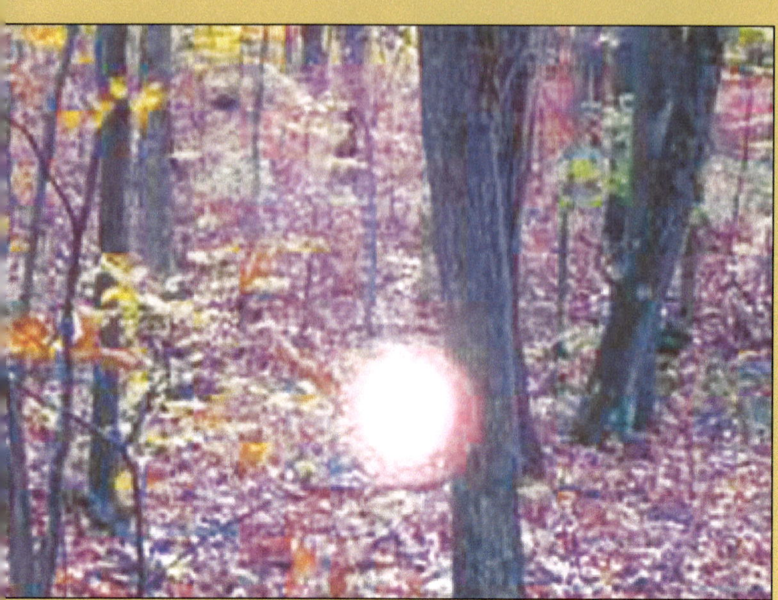

**For the children (or the child in you), QofF means "Queen of the Faeries"—a nickname given to me long ago by a "child-at-heart" friend.*

"Never forget that, no matter how small you feel, anything is possible!"

Denise Crawn is an ordained Interfaith Minister. Her ministry includes "Walking Awake" workshops, retreats, and pilgrimages, helping others to see and sense nature's faces, signs, and connections.

For more information, you can visit her at www.walkingawake.com.